A Better Way to Think About Business

A Better Way
to Think
About Business

How Personal Integrity Leads to Corporate Success

Robert C. Solomon

New York   Oxford
Oxford University Press
1999

Oxford University Press

Oxford   New York

Athens   Auckland   Bangkok   Bogotá   Buenos Aires   Calcutta
Cape Town   Chennai   Dar es Salaam   Delhi   Florence   Hong Kong   Istanbul
Karachi   Kuala Lumpur   Madrid   Melbourne   Mexico City   Mumbai
Nairobi   Paris   São Paulo   Singapore   Taipei   Tokyo   Toronto   Warsaw

and associated companies in

Berlin   Ibadan

Copyright © 1999 by Robert C. Solomon

Published by Oxford University Press, Inc.
198 Madison Avenue, New York, New York 10016

Oxford is a registered trademark of Oxford University Press

Library of Congress Cataloging-in-Publication Data
Solomon, Robert C.
A better way to think about business : how personal integrity
leads to corporate success / Robert C. Solomon.
p.   cm.
Includes bibliographical references and index.
ISBN 0-19-511238-5 (alk. paper)
1. Business ethics.   I. Title.
HF5387   .S612 1999
174' .4- -dc21   98-34297

1 3 5 7 9 8 6 4 2

Printed in the United States of America
on acid-free paper

For some virtuous ethicists who are very good friends:
Tom Donaldson, Ed Freeman, Pat Werhane, Joanne Ciulla,
and Kathy Higgins

Special thanks to
Jenene Allison, Jacqueline Thomas,
and Karen Mottola

Contents

How to Use This Book

This book is, in effect, a program in ethics. I wrote it on the basis of twenty years of working with a variety of companies, including Chase Manhattan Bank, AT&T, NCR, IBM, and Motorola, and meeting tens of thousands of executives and managers who were interested in, intrigued by, suspicious of, or, in a few cases, downright hostile to the idea of ethics in business.

In Walker Percy's classic novel *The Moviegoer*, the businessman hero proclaims, "What good people they are. It is not at all a bad thing to be a businessman. There is a spirit of trust and cooperation here. . . . Everyone jokes about such things, but if businessmen were not trusting of each other the country would collapse tomorrow."

I think that is true. In my years of business consulting, the number of friendly, admirable, virtuous people I have met has been overwhelming. The few crooks and sleazebags have been memorable, to be sure, but mainly because they were out of step with the corporate cultures they blemished by their presence.

But the vast majority of conscientious managers and executives are not self-righteous or overly satisfied with themselves. In fact, they seem to share a widespread discomfort, however enthusiastic and unqualified their praise for the "free enterprise system." They are offended that business too often rewards those of easy virtue. They are threatened and often angry that hard work and integrity no longer guarantee job security and advancement. They resent the fact that they are forced to make hard ethical choices between what they know is right and what the company expects them to do, between the humanly compassionate decision and its cost/benefit alternative.

Executives and managers are often uncomfortable and unprepared for the moral dilemmas they find themselves facing, the very situations that seem not to bother their less scrupulous colleagues. Some of them see the need to face such choices as a poor reflection on themselves. But most of them see them as an obstacle to their "real" work, as if ethics is more a necessary nuisance than the very heart of their responsibilities. My job is not only to help them make such choices but, more importantly, to get them to see these choices and their responsibilities in a different and better light.

In my seminars and in this book, I argue that the way we think about business all too often tends to relegate ethics to the margins, to see morals as a set of side constraints, necessary but tangential to the real-life business of business. The result is that the best people find themselves on the defensive, uncomfortable, and even cynical about what they do for a living. "This business is a jungle" is one familiar expression of this discomfort. Another, less metaphorical, is the lament about "market forces," which pressure people to act in ways of which they themselves would not personally approve. What is easily ignored, or simply overlooked, is that there is a way to think about business that eliminates many of those difficult choices and renders others far less threatening and infuriating. Good executives and managers know—or would like to know—the power of integrity, of having the right values at work, of cultivating virtues on the job that allow one to face up to the most difficult ethical demands and avoid the grueling ethical decisions that come only after a long downward slide in which integrity, values, and virtues have been neglected, compromised, or straightforwardly violated.

Why do good people do not-so-good things? The answer is rarely straightforward, and the slide into unethical and intolerable behavior typically begins step by little step, motivated by resentment and untouched by company policies that would prevent such behavior. How can companies avoid the moral dilemmas (and the lawsuits) that wreak the worst havoc in even the best organizations? By fostering integrity at the very core (and at the very top) of the organization? But even in the most virtuous companies, every manager or executive sometimes feels the tension between doing what is necessary and doing what he or she thinks is right. This is not only personally painful, but it is also bad for business. It leads to inefficiency and distrust. It leads to poor morale, bitterness, and cynicism. And it results in a diminished reputation, both of one's own business and of business in general. Our goal must be to eliminate, or at least minimize, such tensions.

That is what this book is about. In my workshops and seminars, I raise the questions, Where does this discomfort or tension come from? How can it be corrected? Is it necessary to doing business, or is it only the product of a limited and remediable way of thinking? And I answer in terms that most people find congenial: Excellence in business begins with a conception of business activity that is not separated from the *values* that most of us hold dear. But values are effective only insofar as they are built right into one's personal and corporate character. They are not just talk, unwalked. They are not just top-down impositions and spiritually uplifting posters on the walls of the corporate cafeteria. They must become manifested as *virtues*, personally endorsed, and second-nature ways of doing things and thinking about business matters. And to hold this altogether—not opposed to but in collaboration with one's ambitions, affections, fears, and temptations, cultivated in a more or less "natural" and personally fulfilling way of being in the world—is what we call *integrity*.

This is a book about integrity in business life. It is a book about the values and the virtues that constitute integrity, and it is about how integrity gets reinforced and rewarded as well as how it gets compromised, undermined, and distracted. *A Better Way to Think About Business* is a condensation, a distillation, a sharpening, and a clarifying of a philosophy of business and of life that I have been developing over the years, and it is also an updated, much condensed, and more concise version of my earlier book, *Ethics and Excellence* (1991), which, I have been told often enough, helped legitimate the language of virtue in business circles and put "virtue ethics" at the center of ongoing debates in business ethics. *A Better Way to Think About Business* is just that, a better way to think about business. It is an attempt to make this perspective useful to a broad business audience.

The body of the book is divided into three parts. The first part is an exploration of the ways we go wrong in business, through faulty visions and, consequently, the wrong kinds of values. The results are the most pervasive business vices—greed and defensiveness, ruthlessness and the "business is business" rationalization for bad behavior. The function of this part of the book is to remind us of where we have been and of the myths and metaphors that block our sense of integrity.

The second part of the book brings us to the heart of the matter.

It presents a vision of business that is, I would argue, much closer to the vision of the free enterprise system that Adam Smith elegantly defended than the narrow picture of the world often defended in his name. The focus of the section is on integrity and what it means, and how integrity can become the core value of corporate life and corporate leadership at every level. But integrity is not a single virtue or the embodiment of any one value. It is rather a sense of wholeness, a way of tying one's life and one's career together. It gets cultivated and realized in any number of more concrete virtues, including such stalwarts as honesty, trustworthiness, and fairness.

The third part, accordingly, is a working catalog of the virtues in business. For maximum utility, I have presented this in encyclopedia form, with the virtues presented in alphabetical order. That means that there is no need to insist that some virtues are more important than others, which too often results in an overly rigid sense of integrity. It also means that the food for thought and action provided in this part of the book can be dined on in an individually customized way, smorgasbord-style. I encourage the reader to browse and munch at his or her own pace, rather than pursue the virtues "from Ability to Zeal." My purpose is not to present the reader with a formula or recipe for virtue, a pretension I find absurd, but to provide a new and better way of thinking about business, in terms of the virtues and their many combinations and manifestations.

Business is about integrity as well as profits, and the profits mean little if their cost sacrifices integrity. (In other walks of life, this is called "prostitution.") Business serves people and not the other way around, and it is value and virtue that make business life rewarding and meaningful. It is easy to say this, as an abstract philosophy, but it is much more important to make it work in practice.

Introduction: Can Virtue Be Taught?

Twenty years ago, I was invited by a friend to speak to a group of business executives in a special program at the University of Texas. I was a budding young philosophy professor, and quite frankly, I had little business sense or sympathies. I asked my friend, Management Professor Paul Nelson, what I could possibly have to say to these folks who work in the Real World. He responded, encouragingly, that "they would be interested in anything I had to tell them." Well, so they seemed to be, although all that I remember saying was something about money and the meaning of life and the need for transcultural moral understanding.

I've been working with groups of businesspeople and corporations ever since, and I am still talking about the meaning of life and morals in business. But still, before every session with successful executives and managers, I feel a twinge of nervousness: "What will I say to them?" I no longer fear, as I once did, that hard-headed businesspeople would have no interest in ethics. Quite the contrary. I find the level of interest so keen that I fear that I might not be able to satisfy it. They rightly wonder (and sometimes ask), "I am already a moral person, so what do you have to teach me?"

That seems to me to be exactly the right question. I do not have to teach anyone the difference between right and wrong. (Indeed, if I did, I would not know how to go about doing so.) But what bothers virtually every one of my clients, from the CEO of one of New York's largest banks to the welder at our local IBM plant, is how to firm up the connection between the bottom-line demands of business and ethics. And that is something well worth talking about.

Down from the Mountaintop

It is often said, by way of a joke, that "business ethics" is a contradiction in terms, an oxymoron.

To some extent, this only reflects normal skepticism. We have all been cheated by some bad apple auto mechanic or have been taken in by some mail-order scam at some point in our lives. We all know businesses that cut corners, and most of us have been in positions ourselves where our sense of doing right has been pressured or compromised. But I think that the skepticism about business ethics goes deeper than that, into our very way of thinking about both business and ethics.

That is why I begin my seminars with a story about ethics:

> Moses went to the top of the mountain, and there God "handed down" to him a set of Commandments, sanctioned by Himself, most of which begin, "Thou shalt not . . ." Moses turned around, went down the mountain, and handed the Law down to his people, who were not, if you recall, particularly receptive.

This is how we often think about ethics, as "handed down," imposed from above, primarily in the form of prohibitions and constraints. It is an understandable way of thinking about ethics, given how most of us learn about morals in the first place:

> Mother yells, "Stop it! Don't tease your baby brother."
> The older child responds, "Why not?!"
> Mother replies (as she should), "Because I said so!"

Here is ethics "from the top," "handed down" or imposed by a recognized authority (with the power to punish). And so it is natural for us to think of ethics in terms of prohibitions and constraints. But when we think of ethics in this way, whether our response is obedience or rebellion, our ethics is not, in an all-important sense, our own.

Then I tell another story, this one about business:

> The great economist Adam Smith taught us all the power of the law of supply and demand, that free enterprise produces prosperity, but that free enterprise must be, above all, free. The proper attitude of all nonbusiness concerns toward business should be laissez faire, "leave it alone."

Insofar as ethics is thought of as a set of constraints, imposed by the law or other moral authorities, there will be a practical contradiction with business as "free enterprise," by its very nature free from external constraints. But to so think of ethics as constraint and business as free from constraint leads to an impoverishment of both, and it quite naturally gives rise to the following kind of not so unfamiliar story:

> Moe the shyster meets Larry the liquidator, and together they strike up a deal to take over hardworking entrepreneur Curly's business. They fire Curly and all of his employees and sell off the business in pieces. They agree that the ethics are dubious, but "it's legal," and, after all, "business is business."

Business is not free in the sense that it is an amoral, unethical activity. And ethics is not merely a matter of obeying the law or some other set of external constraints. Therefore, what we explore for the next several hours or days, and in this book, is how ethics in business is not only possible but necessary, how markets can be both free and moral, and why "business ethics" is not a contradiction but rather the precondition of any flourishing business enterprise.

The best answer to the charge of contradiction lies in the concept of *virtue*. A virtue, unlike an externally imposed constraint, is very much our own. Our virtues (and vices) make us the persons we are. But virtues, in turn, presuppose *values*. A value simply espoused, even if it is sincerely believed, is worth very little if it is not translated into action. Virtues are values turned into action. Virtues and values come together in *visions* of business and the role of business in life more generally. Our vision dictates our values and informs our virtues, so virtue is not just action. It is intelligent, visionary action, expressing one's sense of what the world must be like. And virtues provide the foundation of both ethical living and success in business.

Back to the Mountain: Living Our Values

Here is another story. It is called "The Parable of the Sadhu"[1]:

> A successful Wall Street banker travels to the Himalayas for a much-needed vacation, to engage in a long-term dream he has had, to trek across one of the world's most challenging mountain passes. He is a religious man. He is an ambitious man.
>
> About halfway up to the pass, he and his group are approached by a group of New Zealanders, who hand over the half-frozen but still living body of a Sadhu, a holy man, who has come down over the pass in the wrong direction and gotten lost in the freezing cold and the snow and ice of the mountain.
>
> If he and his group take the Sadhu down to safety, the wind and snow will close the mountain pass and they will have to give up their attempt. If they do not, he will surely die. One of the group, an anthropologist, decides that the Sadhu must be saved. The banker insists on going over the pass. The anthropologist takes the Sadhu halfway down, then hands him to a group of Japanese, who give him some food but refuse to carry him any farther. The anthropologist then hurries to meet his friend over the pass.
>
> When they join together, the anthropologist angrily asks the banker, "How does it feel to have contributed to the death of another human being?" The banker, surprised, defensively insists, "we all did our bit. There was nothing else we could do. If we had taken him down, the whole trip would have been for nothing!"

Two years later, he wrote a confession of what he did (or did not do) for the most prestigious business journal, for everyone in his world to read.

I ask, What do you make of this story, with regard to business life?

The conversation is almost always brisk and keen. Virtually everyone sees the obvious analogy between "climbing the corporate ladder" (or otherwise pursuing your own personal objectives) and climbing a mountain. They also see an undeniable ethical lapse, an unforgivable neglect of the plight of another human being, in this case, in a life-or-death situation. Several participants talk about the breakdown in teamwork, both between and within the groups, their collective failure to coordinate a rescue effort. No one, but no one, was willing to take on the final responsibility (not even the anthropologist, who found himself caught between his good intention to save the Sadhu and the need to get across the pass and join his friend).

But the discussion turns truly active when the nature of the banker's action (or lack of appropriate action) comes into question. He was not ignorant of the difference between right and wrong, or of the value of human life—perhaps the most important value of all. It was not as if he did not recognize his obligations. But, rather, he was blinded by his own objective, and no doubt by the perseverance that had made him such a success on Wall Street, too. His very virtues became vices, obstacles to his doing what he surely knew he ought to do.

Moreover, he *rationalized*. He found all sorts of reasons why *not* saving the Sadhu was the right (or at least the permissible) thing to do. He insists, for example, that they had made a considerable investment in the trip, in terms of time, effort, and expense.

Indeed they had, as we all make investments in our careers, our projects, our lives. But, sometimes, those investments have to be abandoned or compromised for a greater good, a more important value.

The banker insists that they had their "own safety to think about."

Indeed, they did, but, apart from the normal dangers of mountain trekking, they would not have put themselves in any further danger by taking the Sadhu down the mountain.

The banker complains that their "altitude sickness was getting worse." But the one piece of advice given in every pamphlet, article, or book on mountain climbing regarding altitude sickness is this: *Go down*. Quite the contrary of making the rescue effort more difficult, altitude sickness would seem to provide a motive for the climbers to rescue the Sadhu, thus giving themselves an honorable excuse for giving up the climb and making themselves feel better.

There is also the nasty question of racism that emerges: The anthropologist, now angry, asks the banker, "Would you have behaved in the same way if the victim were a Western woman instead of an exotic stranger?" That in turn raises the tricky question of "relativism," whether one has the obligation to behave according to one's own values when dealing with people whose values may be very different. (One group of bright young MBAS turned the question on its head, demanding, "What right do we have to interfere with the Sadhu's activity, whatever it may have been? Moreover, why should we take responsibility for someone else's irresponsibility?" Hard and important questions indeed.)

But what the story and the discussion illustrate to almost everyone's satisfaction is that believing in values alone is not enough. Values have to be translated into action, and that means acting according to our values cannot merely be an abstract obligation but must be built into our ways of dealing with the world. That is what a virtue is, and that is what good business and business ethics and this book are all about.

Why Virtue Is Necessary

At a recent conference on the environment, a particularly belligerent critic hammered away at "international capital" for degrading the ecology of the planet. The statistics of such degradation are frightening, of course. The ethical and political solutions suggested seemed to me impractical. What fascinated me, however, was that one obvious solution to the problem was never even mentioned, namely, the idea that the multi- and transnational corporations he so abused and accused might themselves feel some sense of obligation to look after the environment. Or, rather, the board and executives and employees and customers of those companies might feel some such obligation. Instead, the corporate world was treated as an impersonal monolith. There were no heroes, just one villain, "international capital."

The speaker lamented that there were no social or political forces available to combat this monolith, and in a sense, what he said was certainly true. But what was wrong was the idea of a monolith in the first place. Quite apart from the question of effective international legal sanctions and monitoring organizations, there is, first and foremost, the question of corporate virtue—the virtues, that is, of all of the people who make up, patronize, and invest in the many different corporations that make up so much of the business world. In the absence of such virtues, I would feel compelled to join the pessimists in worrying desperately about our collective future. But I see such virtues all around the business world, and at all levels. Without such virtues, we would surely enter a new Dark Age. But now we might instead see some semblance of a new world order in which humanity, and not just profits, becomes the measure. The choice is up to us, not to the mindless workings of "international capital."

This tendency to depersonalize, to see corporations as all of a piece, defined by legalities and buried under a handful of economic abstractions, is the target of this book. There is no such thing as "international capital." There is no such entity as "Corporate America." There is only Motorola, AT&T, Chase Manhattan and Citibank, IBM, Compaq and Apple, Merck and Upjohn, Johnson & Johnson, Exxon, Nike, and Freeport-McMoran, or, more accurately, the people who make up these companies. There are, to be sure, a few exemplary good guys and some despicable bad guys, but there are thousands of companies and many millions of executives, managers, and employees who are neither saints nor monsters but just people trying to live a decent, happy life and doing their jobs accordingly. Corporations are not faceless forces or monoliths. We have to remind and convince ourselves that they are nothing but people and relationships, flesh and blood, working together in cooperation and mutual self-interest, trying—most of them—to do the right thing.

Problematic, too, is that abstraction called *the market* ("the institutionalization of irresponsibility," in the delicious phrase of the great "Buddhist" economist, E.F. Schumacher). The market may be the product of our collective psychology, but it is not, obviously, within our personal control. Even the most powerful among us feels constrained and powerless in the face of market forces. But what tends to get left out of the picture is our own free will and responsibility. As employees and managers, as consumers and stockholders, we are always making choices, and as we choose, we create ourselves. We build reputations as we display our virtues and our vices. The foundation of free enterprise is not the iron laws of economics but the personal question, "Who are you, and what do you (really) want?" Whether addressed to one individual or a multinational corporation with a hundred thousand employees and managers, we want to know: "What are your virtues, and why should we trust and support you?" It is my purpose here to define and defend those virtues, right in the bowels of business.

The problems of business today are, first and foremost, profoundly ethical and philosophical problems. They are questions about the very nature of the business enterprise and the nature of the corporation. For example, the very conception of the corporation as a "legal fiction" defined in terms of obligations to its stockholders implies that corporations are not moral or morally responsible agencies and suggests (at best) a morally ambiguous sense of responsibility for the executives and employees of the corporation. It is not surprising, then, that some major, once respectable companies find themselves riddled and ruined by scandals in which the rubber check of corporate responsibility bounces up and down the hierarchy and seems to get cashed out nowhere.

So, too, business activity itself is misconceived in an amoral way, subsumed (or hidden) under the all-purpose imagery of *competitiveness*. But competition is but one of a large number of relationships that people and companies have with one another, and an overemphasis on competition can be disastrous for the sense of community and for the underlying cooperation that is necessary for any successful business activity. The need to be more competitive is more often than not better cast as the need to be more cooperative, to earn the loyalty, trust, and understanding of one's customers, employees, and investors.

The combination of our amoral conception of the corporation and our emphasis on competition, however, is doubly disastrous, feeding a frenzy of self-serving but (for the corporations and communities involved) ruinous attacks on corporate stability and the personal security of employees. Its results are short-term thinking and an impoverished sense of meaning, inevitable distrust, loss of productivity, and poor employee morale. Ethics, to put the matter bluntly, is good business. Amorality, by contrast, just won't sell in the long run.

In this book, I stress the importance of personal virtues and integrity, but let me be very clear about this: Whatever else it may be, virtue is bound to culture, to politics, to institutions. The ancient Greeks used to say, "To lead a good life and to be a good person, one must live in a great city." Today, despite globalization and the dramatic revolution in communications, that wisdom does not change. In the corporate world, to lead a good life and to be a good person, it is essential to work for a great corporation—great not just in the sense glossily celebrated in the Annual Report, but great in the sense of great to work for, great to be a part of, great in a sense that speaks to our pride and our spirituality, and not just to our pocketbooks.

How we do business—and what business does to us—has everything to do with how we think about business, talk about business, conceive of business, practice business. If we think, talk, conceive, and practice business as a ruthless, cutthroat, dog-eat-dog activity, then that, of course, is what it will become. And so, too, it is what we will become, no matter how often (in our off hours and personal lives) we insist otherwise. If, on the other hand, business is conceived—as it has often been conceived—as an enterprise based on trust and mutual benefits, an enterprise for civilized, virtuous people, then that, in turn, will be equally self-fulfilling. It will also be much more amiable, secure, enjoyable, and, last but not least, profitable.

It is undeniable that a person becomes what he or she does. We are molded by our peers, by the rigors and language of our jobs, by the culture of the organization or the industry. This is not to deny personal choices and responsibility, but it is to say the obvious: If you spend (more than) half of your adult waking life working, including the most creative hours of most of your days, what you do, the people you work with, and the values of the organization you work for are going to be an inescapable influence on who and what you are. (And consider how much of the other half of your life is taken up by travel to and from work, trips to the supermarket or the dry cleaner, emergency visits to the vet, cleaning up the basement, disciplining the kids, mindlessly watching television, personal grooming, not to mention the work you take home with you, etc.) Like it or not, in the modern corporate world, you are—or become—what you do.

In place of the brutally competitive and disruptive imagery and bottom-line thinking that are so pervasive in business these days, I want to underscore the importance of integrity. It may be true, as pundits from Alvin Toffler to Tom Peters have suggested, that most of us will have a half-dozen or more careers in our working lifetimes. But it does not follow from this that the transition from career to career needs to be as utterly traumatic and disruptive, as threatening to mental health and the well-being of families and whole communities as it now tends to be. The way to a future without "future shock," as Toffler calls it, is the main theme of ethics, remembering who we are, what we really need, and what we stand for. What endures, what keeps us whole, is integrity.

An Aristotelian Approach to Business

At the risk of scaring off some of my readers, let me say that the approach to business and business ethics I will be advocating in these pages is an Aristotelian approach, in honor of the great Greek philosopher Aristotle. This, despite the fact that, twenty-five hundred years ago, Aristotle attacked commercial activity as un"natural." Aristotle's mistake (with two millennia of hindsight) was to generalize his indictment of some shrewd financial practices to virtually all of what we call business. It would be even more of a mistake, however, to dismiss Aristotle as irrelevant to the contemporary business world.

The bottom line of the Aristotelian approach to business ethics is that we have to get away from bottom-line thinking and conceive of business as an essential part of the good life. Living well means getting along with others, having a sense of self-respect, and being part of something one can be proud of. Not that Aristotle was against wealth and comfort (no ascetics, those Athenians), but in the quest for the good life, money wasn't the only concern.

The Aristotelian approach to business ethics begins with two concepts, the individual embedded in the community and the ultimate importance of happiness as the sole criterion for success. The good life, according to Aristotle, is the happy life, the flourishing life, "doing well." The point is not that we should stop thinking about money or trying to make a living. It is a question of perspective, and a question of what that living amounts to. Is it, in fact, just a means to make money? Or is it, as it should be, a worthwhile activity that provides the meaningful substance of our adult lives, the source of our sense of self-worth, and where we meet our closest friends? Is the company we work for a white-collar version of hell, or is it a community where we are glad to see our colleagues and get on with the work of the day?

It was Aristotle who insisted on the virtues, or "excellences," as the basic constituents of individual and collective happiness. The underlying assumption was that a person is who he or she is by virtue of his or her place and role in the community, and the virtues of the community, in turn, nurture and encourage each of its members to be a good person. It takes only a little leap of philosophical imagination to recognize this same relationship between the individual employee, manager, or executive and the modern corporation. On the Aristotelian approach to business, a good corporation is one that is not only profitable but that provides a morally rewarding environment in which good people can develop not only their skills but also their virtues.

A Better Way to Think About Business

PART I

How Not to Think About Business
Myths and Metaphors

> We reveal ourselves in the metaphors we choose.
> —Stephen Jay Gould[2]

Marketing 101

Every discipline or profession has its own self-glorifying vocabulary. It is how its proponents justify themselves, sell themselves, and think of themselves and what they do.

▲ Politicians bask in the concept of public service even while they pursue personal power and exploit the fears and prejudices of their constituents. But who would question the virtue of devoting oneself to public service?

▲ Lawyers defend justice and our rights on a handsome contingency basis as they lead us through a thicket of regulations and liabilities created by other lawyers. But who would question the virtue of devoting oneself to justice and rights?

▲ Physicians (even those with bulging portfolios) heal and save lives, an undeniably noble cause. Who would question the value of human life and well-being?

▲ University professors immodestly celebrate what they do in the noble language of truth and knowledge even when they spend most of their time and energy battling one another for status in exquisitely petty but vicious campus politics. But who would question their dedication to the truth, to enlightening young minds, and to preserving the values of civilization?

In the case of business, however, the language of self-description is hardly noble or self-glorifying. One of my businessman friends told me, "In business you always know how well you are doing. You just have to put your hand in your pocket." (I did not pursue the ambiguity of the suggestion.) The simple phrase "the bottom line" and the vulgar verb *making money* summarize a one-dimensional image of business that is notoriously unflattering and, in the public perception, extremely destructive.

We can readily understand why we should applaud people who devote themselves to public service, or defend our rights, or cure illness and save lives, or search for truth and knowledge. It is not so easy to understand why we should cheer for those who (as they themselves seem to claim) are out only for material gain for themselves. There is more than enough cynicism in the world about the callous attitudes in business. Businesspeople themselves should be loathe to confirm such cynicism. One can put as much faith as one wishes in Adam Smith's "invisible hand" and the theory that individual self-interest yields collective prosperity, but it does not follow that we should describe what we do in business merely as making money.

The Language of Dehumanization

In my seminars, I ask, "If someone presented you with $10 million (tax-free), no strings attached, what would you do?" The point is to eliminate money as a consideration, the need to make a living, to get to the real values and interests that motivate us in what we do. How do we feel about our jobs? Are they a source of meaning and self-identity? Or is our job a drudge, a demeaning burden that we would just as soon be rid of? Would we keep working even if our pay became practically irrelevant? (Most people begin by saying no, but with a few minutes of discussion they start to reconsider.) What would we do in our jobs if we had the resources such that we did not have to worry about money? What would we miss about our jobs if we left them? (Almost everyone says, "The people I've worked with.") What gets highlighted here are all of those goals and purposes that have been operative all along but are too easily eclipsed by the need to make money. When someone cannot see the point of working except for that limited reason, it is pathetic. What they are doing, then, is meaningless to them.

The sad truth is that the image of making money—an image of materialistic selfishness—too easily eclipses the many virtues of business and people in business, their dedication to their work and their companies, their surprising selflessness in facing the job to be done, their pride in their products and services, and their relationships with colleagues and customers. It is the "art of the deal" that gets celebrated, not the production and distribution of quality (even lifesaving) goods and services. It is the windfall profit, the "killing" in the market, the outfoxing of the competition, the cost-cutting and ax-to-the-max downsizing that make reputations and headlines, not the routine addition of jobs, the satisfaction of jobs well done, the camaraderie within the corporation, the unpaid (but not unrewarded) compensations of integrity.

Talking about money is one of many ways of dehumanizing business. The great German sociologist–philosopher Georg Simmel speculated about the "impersonality" of money at the beginning of twentieth-century capitalism. Money is peculiar, Simmel wrote, in that it is presented to us, by definition, as free of any attachments, whether sentimental or moral. It is simply a "medium of exchange." There is no morality of money.

In thinking this way, however, we too easily tend to reduce business to an unsentimental, amoral activity. What we leave out are all of those personal attachments and obligations that surround and ultimately give meaning to our financial dealings, our work, and our communal lives. To dehumanize human activity is to forget that real flesh-and-blood human beings, with feelings and families, with real cares and concerns, are not only the agents of the activity but its beneficiaries and its reason for being. If money means something to us, then it is because we endow money and making money with meaning. And where there is meaning, morality cannot be far behind.

When we dehumanize talk about business, we should not be surprised that we face dehumanizing policies, strategies, and institutions in business. In many ways, business is an exemplary human activity, involving as it does mutual attention to needs, desires and demands, creative and productive activity, face-to-face negotiation, acknowledgment of certain rules of fair play, and the importance of trust and keeping one's word. When we talk about business as something less than fully human, or as degrading, then these virtues and concerns are lost from view and may even seem irrelevant.

Again and again we hear business described as a jungle, a fight for survival, a dog-eat-dog world, a game defined by its so-called winners and losers. A casual glance during take-off through the executive-oriented advertisements in any airline or business magazine should be enough to convince anyone how pervasive these images and metaphors are. The concept of competition is used to assault, to terrify, and, of course, to sell products. The all-important concept of fair and mutually stimulating competition gets lost in blood-and-guts survival metaphors.

Metaphors are not just, as one of our more popular publications puts it, "more picturesque speech." They define the way we live, the way we think. They are definitive of the world in which we project ourselves.

An advertisement (for a telephone beeper) portrays the shadows of a wolf and a rabbit on the wall behind two executives (the executive who didn't buy the beeper is the rabbit). Andrew Grove, the CEO of one of the world's most successful companies, has written a self-admittedly "paranoid" account of his own successes in the guerrilla wars of Silicon Valley.[3] Bill Gates, under attack from the US Justice Department, keeps insisting that his company's very survival is at stake. No one denies that business competition can be rough stuff, that one does at critical moments reach "strategic inflection points" in which a business, a career, or an industry may survive or fail.

These are the moments that test our ultimate ability to cope and to survive, but failing such tests is not the end of the story. Not only can failure make us better human beings, but it can improve our chances for future success. (This is not true of the rabbit that fails to escape the wolf.)

To think of passing such tests as the sole reason for being in business in the first place is not very different from being one of those awful students who sees the only purpose in taking a course as a way to pass the test at the end of it. Either the course should not be taken (or given) at all, or the student has missed the real point of the course (and, perhaps, of his or her education).

If we actually believed the self-descriptions of business activity as Darwinian survivalism and jungle warfare, we as a society would be quite properly justified in wanting to outlaw business as brutal and uncivilized behavior that served no social purpose. The ritualistic incantation of Adam Smith's "invisible hand" saves the game only momentarily. There are limits to what we as a society will tolerate, even with the promise of future prosperity. Adam Smith, in particular, would have no patience for these dehumanizing metaphors, and for him, business is defensible just because it is among the most human and the most social of activities. One would not know this from the way businesspeople talk about themselves and what they do.

We hear too little about the virtues of business life, about the ways in which business and personal integrity support and reinforce one another, perhaps because it makes for such boring and uneventful stories—just modest success and good feelings, camaraderie, mutual pride, and enjoyment. Indeed, it sometimes seems as if virtue and integrity—not to mention productivity and general prosperity—have been reduced to mere means to profitability. This is the most common dehumanization of business, putting profits before (and even in the place of) people. But this is not the worst of it.

Attila the Hun and Other Business Heroes

Just as every discipline has its own self-glorifying vocabulary, it also has its heroes, its role models, those who are admired from afar, looked up to and emulated. Politicians have their Washington, their Lincoln, their Roosevelts, their Churchill. Lawyers have Clarence Darrow, and physicians and nurses their Hippocrates, Jonas Salk, Florence Nightingale. University professors sing the praises of Einstein, Socrates, and occasionally a more prestigious version of "Mr. Chips." But in business, we have a cascade of best-selling books lauding the management "secrets" of Attila the Hun and Machiavelli. They are full of enthusiasm for "Sun-Tze" (the art of war), but they neglect his compatriot Confucius, who knows the real "secret" of Asian prosperity: *virtue*, integrity, and a real sense of community.

This is a phenomenon worth scrutinizing, if only because it highlights a pathology that has come to infect so much of business thinking. Take, for example, Wess Roberts's *Leadership Secrets of Attila the Hun*, published in 1989 with rave comments from presidential contender Ross Perot ("a great book") and management guru Tom Peters ("fantastic!"). Attila became "a managerial cult classic" (according to *Forbes* magazine), and Roberts followed this success with a sequel, *Victory Secrets of Attila the Hun* in 1993.[4] Both books are filled with a mix of insightful if one-sided historical commentary and management commonplaces dressed up in the language of "tribes, chieftains, warriors and battle." For instance, "Chieftains [managers] accomplish greater feats when they focus their warriors and Huns [employees] on tribal rather than individual goals."[5]

The appeal of the books, one surmises, and all that distinguishes it from standard management fare, is the overt use of unabashed warrior language. And, of course, the enduring mystique of Attila, who ranks just below fictional Conan the Barbarian and slightly above the very real Genghis Khan in terms of his horrible reputation. Roberts seduces readers with Attila's bloodthirsty image, but he is too civilized to leave the sword unsheathed. Thus he dutifully repudiates the corporate equivalent of any type of bloodthirsty behavior and condemns, for example, "predatory inclination" because it "can develop into sadistic gratification." He criticizes those "insecure chieftains" who pick on wounded Huns "instead of helping them heal,"[6] a Christian sentiment that certainly would have been foreign to the real Attila and his chieftains.

But even without questioning the wisdom of such "secrets," we should certainly question Roberts's choice of a managerial role model. Attila as business hero? How readily columnists for *The Nation* or *The Progressive* would agree with that comparison.

Attila was known in his time as "the scourge of God." He was known for his cruelty, for causing widespread death and destruction. He himself evidently took considerable delight in crushing babies and murdering pregnant women.

He openly encouraged vandalism, meaning not graffiti and a few smashed windows but the looting, burning, and murder of whole cities. (The word "vandalism" refers to the Vandals, a tribe with whom Attila early allied himself. The historian H.A.L. Fisher writes of them, "The Vandals were savages. They destroyed much, they created nothing. In their hundred years of rule only memories of havoc remain."[7]) Attila decimated Venetia and the Balkans, and although he was finally devastated in Gaul, he was nevertheless instrumental in the destruction of the Roman Empire and much of what is now celebrated as "Western civilization."

Now, what does it say of a civilized modern executive that he should take such a character as a guide to business strategy? And what does it say about business, that it honors such "heroes"?

I don't deny that there are "tips" to be gleaned even from monsters. (Are we lacking Hitler's "management secrets" only because he so recently lost the war?) But one should distinguish learning a trick or two from taking on a new hero or role model. Imagine an ordinary citizen, listening to such barbarians talk about themselves and their conquests. What would one think? What would one do? Would one wish them well? Trust them unfettered and unregulated? Support their interests before Congress?

One can know a good deal about a person by knowing whom he or she admires. Someone who admires and emulates the historical Jesus or Socrates tells us something about the place of faith, truth, and nonviolent courage in his or her life. Someone who admires Einstein or Picasso similarly lets us know about what he or she sees as the importance of cosmic vision or creativity.

On the other hand, people who admire Hitler or Stalin strike us as loathesome. They represent megalomania, intrigue and betrayal, lethal prejudices, demagoguery, subversion, cruelty, and genocide. To be sure, the greatest crimes become mere anecdotes when sufficiently distant in history, but the idea of whitewashing and celebrating Hitler or Stalin a thousand years from now should still strike us as intolerable in its bad taste and lack of historical sensitivity.

To hold up the "scourge of God" as a leadership hero, to cast him as a role model in business, is surely to set ourselves up for a world that we could only loathe.

"Better Fear Than Love"

Self-proclaimed realists will tell you that the world is a rough place, that life is unfair, and that only the ruthless survive. But what they call "real" is only the projection of their own bad faith.

Consider Niccolò Machiavelli, who, unlike Attila, did not kill anyone. He was, in effect, a brilliant consultant, but like most consultants, he was careful to tell his client, the Prince, what he wanted to hear and what he could use with more or less immediate results. There is good evidence that Machiavelli in fact thought very little of his client's ambitions or virtues, and perhaps he wrote *The Prince* tongue-in-cheek. But Anthony Jay takes him seriously in his *Management and Machiavelli*.[8] So does Harriett Rubin in her delightfully scandalous recent book, *The Princessa*, who playfully remakes the Machiavellian model for the modern-day business-woman.[9] Machiavelli, it is clear, is in vogue in business.

In historical perspective, however, we should be appalled at the changes that Machiavelli (and other Renaissance philosophers) loosed upon the world. What they replaced, in particular, was Aristotle's conception of the honorable statesman, the melding of ethics and politics, the coupling of virtue and living well. Instead, they fanned the flames of self-interest, pure selfishness, a "war of all against all" (in the words of Thomas Hobbes, one of Machiavelli's best-known English colleagues). [10]

To look to the famously corrupt, murderous, and intrigue-filled courts of sixteenth-century Italy for insights into twenty-first-century management problems is surely to adopt a tragically mistaken historical paradigm. It is, in short, just the paradigm of corrupt central control, manipulation, and mutual sabotage—without any attention whatever to the customer—that Adam Smith and the free enterprise movement sought to replace.

Because of the corruption and intrigue, Italy was and would remain the basket case of Western Europe. At a time when England, Spain, Holland, and France were beginning the great explorations that would soon make them the most powerful nations in the world, the Italian princes were busy poisoning one another. (It is worth noting that the most famous Italian explorer, Christopher Columbus, crossed the Atlantic under a Spanish flag.) When the industrial revolution and the Enlightenment were transforming the face of Europe, the Dominican monk Savonarola wrote of his superiors, "They are worse than the Turks and the Moors. Their greed is insatiable."

The Italy of Machiavelli's time was hardly a model of the healthy corporation. The country was fragmented into hundreds of warring states. Rome was a sinkhole of depravity, corruption, and vice. Whatever the remaining power of the pope, Rome had lost its moral authority, and the Reformation was just around the corner. (Talk about not anticipating the competition!) Whatever Machiavelli's genius, his princes and their realms are hardly the model for an aspiring contemporary executive or corporation.

Again, it is not the historical details that should interest us here but the question of self-image and identity. Do we want to put our trust in someone who proclaims that his leadership is based on Machiavelli's principles? Would an employee be impressed by and loyal to a boss who believed, as Machiavelli famously writes, "Tis better to rule through fear than love"? Or isn't that the infamous "boss from hell"? Would you want to do business with someone who was described to you as "Machiavellian"? Why do we honor, even celebrate, such behavior?

Given that the principles of good leadership and management are more or less perennial, despite the new vocabularies and buzzwords that populate the monthly fashions and best-sellers, do we really want to take our cues and hitch our reputations to the most vicious and corrupt societies in history?

What do we think of ourselves—adolescents trying to be shocking?—when we take pleasure in accepting such identifications?

This is Gangsta rap for executives, hardly a recipe for success in business.

Masters of the Universe

That there are modern-day Attilas and Machiavellis is obvious, and the same uncritical admiration is in evidence. Michael Milken, whatever your view of the market he created, was lionized as "Master of the Universe" and as a king (of junk bonds, but a king nevertheless). The business and popular press variously bemoaned and celebrated his fall, but the cynical public he left in his wake remains as evidence of the cost of having such people as heroes.

Michael Ovitz, the "Master of the Deal" and "Hollywood's Most Powerful Man," flunked out of Disney World. While establishing his myth of invincibility and making millions for himself, he engineered such global failures as the merger of Columbia Pictures and SONY and MCA with Matsushita.[11] Nevertheless, he remained the much-feared idol of the make-believe world of Hollywood and the model for any number of Ovitz-wanna-bes.

In place of horses and swords, the new barbarian does battle with a cellular phone in a limo, but the archetype remains the same. Clout is the sole virtue; power is character. This is not to deny either Milken's or Ovitz's talents, but it is to question the uncritical hero worship that is all too much a part of the business world. Curiously, the problem in the rest of America seems to be the utter lack of heroes, if we discount the utterly inappropriate pantheon of entertainment and sports stars. Heroes are supposed to be role models, exemplars of excellence. What are we settling for instead?

Here is a different role model for executives. He is not historical but very contemporary. He did not murder anyone, and he did not end up going to prison or being exiled from the kingdom after months of rumor and intrigue. No doubt, therefore, his story does not make titillating reading. He is Aaron Feuerstein, who was and is CEO of Malden Mills, a textile company in Massachusetts.

Just before Christmas 1995, a fire destroyed the manufacturing plant in Lawrence, Massachusetts, and three thousand employees were put out of work. Feuerstein announced that he would keep all of them on payroll while the business was being rebuilt, and in January, and again in February, he continued to pay them and assure them of jobs. The plant was back in full operation by March, and, needless to say, Malden Mills now has the most loyal, hardworking workers around.[12]

Feuerstein is not the usual candidate for business hero. He has no pretensions of being a "master of the universe." He is just a very successful businessman and human being. I doubt that "The Management Secret of Malden Mills"—namely, "We consider our workers an asset, not an expense"—would ever have the caché of *Attila* or *The Prince*, but that, perhaps, is the shame of it. True, Feuerstein paid out several million dollars that others might have seen as "unnecessary," but in the "long run" (about six months!), Malden Mills came out just fine. Feuerstein is known for other such unnecessary "perks," for instance, arranging a couple of heart operations for employees, but we are rarely surprised when one virtuous action goes hand in hand with any number of other virtuous actions and attitudes. (Conversely, would we really expect that Attila, behind his "scourge of God" reputation, was really a nice guy to work for?)

Feuerstein's management ideas include such taking-care-of-business secrets as "the quality of our product is paramount," and "it's the employee who makes quality." This is not the embattled wisdom of *Victory Secrets of Attila the Hun*, but then why is it so common that business leaders wear the masks of the military rather than the sensitive faces of those who care about people and effectively take care of their own?

We should broaden this set of questions: Why are hostile takeovers considered good business, whereas taking care of employees is considered softhearted and unbusinesslike? There is much evidence showing that the brutality in business in the past decade or so had catastrophic effects on employee morale and productivity. Corpo rations that do not engage in these practices, on the other hand, have shown consistent and spectacular long-term profitability, not to mention the immeasurable sense of well-being and pride of employees and the satisfaction of all their customers.

How much damage do we do to ourselves when we celebrate only the high fliers of finance and ignore or deny the ordinary heroes who take care of their employees and still make a handsome profit? Just good solid people doing good, important jobs.

Metaphors of Mayhem, Visions of Civility

The battlefield is the metaphorical equivalent of the marketplace.
—Wess Roberts, *Victory Secrets of Attila the Hun*[13]

I have long been disturbed by the gap in the corporate world between the polite, friendly faces and conversations in the offices of flourishing corporations and the truly frightening images that get thrown around once the conversation gets more free-floating and abstract. "It's a jungle out there." "It's kill or be killed." Of course, some political infighting occurs in almost every organization, and in the business world, not every company survives. But bankruptcy today is rarely fatal, and however horrible six months of unemployment may be, it hardly compares with the war victim/refugee images invoked on its behalf.

How a person thinks about business—as a ruthless competition for profits or as a cooperative enterprise whose aim is the prosperity of the community—preshapes much of his or her behavior and attitudes toward fellow employees or executives, competitors, customers, and the surrounding community. Business is full of philosophy, although not necessarily good philosophy. Business is defined by its ethics, and businesspeople, by their virtues. But the philosophy that makes it onto the business pages of many newspapers is appalling, and the business virtues most often celebrated are not really virtues at all.

Thirty years ago, Alfred Carr made his name in business ethics circles when he published one of the most often refuted articles in the field. Carr argued at length that business is a lot like poker and (therefore) does not follow the rules of ordinary morality.[14] But as the infuriated comments poured into the *Harvard Business Review*, it became apparent that the object of indignation was not Carr's game analogy but rather his choice of games.

Poker is often viewed as disreputable and primarily a vehicle for gambling. Had Carr chosen football, he probably would have won unanimity (though he would have failed to create such a controversy, obviously his intent). Indeed, one would almost surmise that the competition for the best business metaphors is akin to a barroom contest to find the least flattering, most offensive, and most unethical image for business life and the business world. As Karl Marx might have said to some corporate pundits today, "With friends like you, who needs Marxists?"

The very phrase "I'm a businessman" has become a warning sign in popular culture. In the 1950s, businessmen on the new medium of television were virtually all crooks or incompetents. In Francis Ford Coppola's blockbuster movie *The Godfather*, one of the most cold-blooded characters proclaims, "I'm a businessman, and blood is bad for business."[15] In the action movie *Eraser*, good guy Arnold Schwarzenegger confronts his boss (played by James Caan), who argues in defense of his brutal actions, "I'm a businessman. I'm a very, very serious businessman."

How we talk reflects how we think, and how we think affects how we act and the nature of the organizations and institutions we create for ourselves. If we talk like brutes and we think like brutes, we will act like brutes and build organizations suitable only for brutes. To be sure, even in such organizations, some people will prosper, but life for most of them will be nasty, brutish, and short.

"It's a Jungle Out There!"

Among the most damaging myths and metaphors in business talk are those Darwinian concepts of "survival of the fittest" and "it's a jungle out there." The underlying idea, of course, is that life in business is competitive, and that it isn't always fair. But those two points are very different from the "dog-eat-dog" and "every man for himself" images that are routine in the business world. It is true that business is and must be competitive, but it is not true that it has to be cutthroat or cannabalistic or that "one does whatever it takes to survive."

Of course, some of the animal metaphors are charming: A nice boss is a "teddy bear" and a tough negotiator is a "tiger," but most of them are demeaning. Employees, executives, and competitors are described as snakes in the grass, rats and a wide variety of other rodents, and insects and arachnids. Corporations in turn are described as fish tanks, shark-infested waters, and snake pits, as well as the botanical image of the jungle.

But besides being bad biology (and unfair to the beasts), the jungle metaphors are particularly bad for business, which is (or should be) anything but uncivilized and devoid of rules or fairness. However competitive a particular industry may be, it always rests on a foundation of shared interests and mutually agreed-upon rules of conduct. Competition takes place not in a jungle but in a well-ordered society that it both serves and depends upon.

Business life, unlike life in the mythological jungle, is fundamentally *cooperative*. It is only within the bounds of mutually shared concerns that competition is possible. In fact, evolutionary theory shows that cooperation is almost always the best strategy, even in nature. One of the primary principles of evolution seems to be the evolution of cooperation, from the simplest multicelled organisms to the seemingly ineradicable colonies of ants, termites, and bees; the efficient packs and herds of carnivores and their prey; and, hardly to be left out of this impressive sociobiological portrait, ourselves. Contrary to the "every man for himself" metaphor, business almost always involves large cooperative and mutually trusting groups that include networks of suppliers, service people, customers, and investors.

Business is competitive, by its very nature. But not all

competition is vicious, and nature is by no means so "red in tooth and claw" as our popular metaphors would make it sound. Indeed, what is central to the jungle metaphor is the image of a scenario utterly unconstrained, of animals and plants in a constant battle for survival, against the environment, with one another. But business is one of the most constrained of all human activities. The restrictions on securities trading, for example, are far more exquisite than the not-so-subtle rules and regulations governing most popular sports and hobbies. And these restrictions come not so much from the outside but from the traders and brokers themselves, as necessary conditions for a flourishing marketplace.

It is a point often made by poets and biologists: A human being deprived of a community and a culture is a pathetic, virtually helpless animal.[16] Our comparatively gigantic brain is of relatively little value without the hand-me-downs of successive generations and the ability to cooperate and organize through language. It would be odd indeed if one of the most dramatic contributions to human evolution was a business miniworld in which the accumulated benefits of millions of years have been set aside in favor of a self-destructive intraspecies competition that most of the animal world has more wisely set aside.

"Business as a Battlefield"

> "Business is War."
> —Michael Crichton, *Rising Sun*[17]

War, a familiar metaphor in so many corporate boardrooms ("the war room"), conjures up more bloody imagery than Darwinian theory. Animals in the state of nature spend most of their time playing, relaxing, spending quality family time with their cubs, grazing, or digesting their last meal. Not so for soldiers in a state of readiness for war.

The war metaphor feeds on our collective insecurity. Few of us as individuals would initiate a violent conflict, but put us together in groups, add some rationalization and, perhaps, an aggressive CEO, and what is unthinkable on an individual level becomes all too seductive. Thus we read, as a matter of casual business reporting:

City-Search, with a host of competitors poised to storm the same market, has a guerilla-style battle plan: infiltrate cities before competitors do, co-opt the populace by hiring locally, then mobilize the indigenous powers-that-be to provide content for the Web site.[18]

Such metaphors may get the blood boiling, but just as often, they are self-destructive and, in most cases, just plain silly.[19]

War is perhaps the worst of the dehumanizing images that we impose on ourselves in business. The militaristic notion of protecting your turf, for example, is a particularly bad way of talking about customers. When you protect turf instead of look after the customer, you lose precisely what you are so obsessed to retain.

Military ethicist Anthony Hartle suggests that the military perspective and consequently military metaphors are intrinsically nationalistic, alarmist, pessimistic, conservative, and authoritarian.[20] This has grim implications for the mental health of a productive organization. Paranoia is not usually conducive to creativity or competitiveness.

Geofferey James retells the story of DEC's losing battle with Novell for the networking market. DEC's management thought entirely in warlike metaphors—"business as a battlefield"—and they "fought" against Novell accordingly. Novell, on the other hand, saw the market as an expandable ecosystem, and they won precisely because they did not think of themselves as fighting a war.[21]

Supreme Court Justice Louis Brandeis wrote that "competition consists in trying to do things better than someone else; that is, making or selling a better article at a lesser cost, or otherwise giving better service. It is not a competition to resort to methods of the prize ring, and simply 'knock the other man out.' That is killing a competitor."[22] No business succeeds simply by eliminating the competition, and no manager or executive ever succeeded simply by destroying his or her rivals. All too often, a company wages war against its competitors only to find that it has grown unresponsive to the market or that the market has moved elsewhere. Executives at war with one another find out too late the destructive effects of their rivalry on everyone who works with them, and the jobs they fought for may well not exist anymore. The bitterest battles in business typically end as lose-lose scenarios. The greatest success stories are not war stories at all.

"An Efficient Money-Making Machine"

Although it is less blood-curdling and less violent, the machine metaphor may be even more dehumanizing—and therefore more destructive—than either the jungle or the war metaphor. As the quintessentially impersonal metaphor, the machine metaphor transforms everything human into something cold and mechanical. Emotions, affections, and relationships disappear, to be replaced by mere causes and effects. Corporations are no longer to be identified with the people and personalities that make them up but with the system in which people are replaceable parts and in which personality serves (at best) as a lubricant or (at worst) as grist and inefficiency. The business world as a whole ceases to become a matter of human aspiration and is reduced to market mechanisms. One needs only to take a quick look at current business lingo to see how entrenched such metaphors have become in our discussion of the market, of corporations, and of business in general.

The notion of "reengineering," for example, captures in a word what is wrong with so much of our current thinking about business.[23] (I note the correlative renaming of corporate trainers as "performance engineers," and I wonder whether I am soon to become an "ethics engineer.") By reengineering a corporation, it is made more "efficient." There is no need to mention lives stymied or ruined, the loss of morale, the increase in fear, and, among older employees, the sense of betrayal, and concepts such as loyalty need never arise. (Do we expect the carburetor to be loyal to the engine? And what does the engine owe to the carburetor in return?) Employees and managers are, after all, "human resources," to be replenished as needed. Is anyone surprised, then, when those "resources" get resentful?

The machine metaphor is left over from the eighteenth century, when Adam Smith wrote his great treatise on economics and virtually every theorist in every discipline was still under the spell of the genius Isaac Newton, whose theories in physics had revolutionized modern thinking only a century before.[24] William Paley, a famous theologian, tried to prove the existence of God by drawing the analogy between the wondrous design of nature and the carefully designed machinery of a watch. So, too, the dream of the social philosophers was to design a society that operated with similar order and efficiency according to mechanisms such as those described in Newton's theories. Adam Smith's best friend, David Hume, tried to develop a theory of human nature according to the same mechanical model that explained the motions of the stars and the machinery of nature. Of course, it was also about this time that the industrial revolution was beginning in Britain, and machines were quite properly perceived as man-made miracles.

It is easy to see how the machine metaphor would still appeal to corporate planners and managers, even two centuries after the metaphor has lost its caché in virtually every other line of thinking (Indeed, even in physics and engineering the machine metaphor has been replaced by more organic, statistical, and holistic metaphors.) Corporations are supposed to "run smoothly." The parts are all supposed to work together, and the gears to be well oiled. The ideal is *efficiency*, a notion borrowed for business directly from Newtonian physics.

Employees are cogs in a great machine, just as all of us and every corporation too are cogs in even greater machines, the national and global economies, whose efficiency and operation can be measured by those mind-boggling numbers released every month by this or that government bureau or department. Thus corporations become money machines ("cash cows" represent one of the few slips into biology here), and management—whatever more fashionable theory provides the facade—is by the numbers. Profits are the product, and the machine that produces them—which, by the way, also produces products or provides services as well as a social environment for its interchangeable employees—is well designed and well run. If not, it needs to be "reengineered" for better efficiency.

Those who think of business or businesses in this way are too often caught up in the idea of control. But control itself might be said to be the core of the problem.

Control is the very antithesis of trust, and trust lies at the heart of every human cooperative relationship. Control is also the antithesis of creativity. It stifles innovation because it shifts the focus from what one might do to what one must do. Control is also the antithesis of autonomy. People cannot think for themselves so long as someone else is thinking for them. And control sits uncomfortably with participation. Why take part if the outcome is mechanically predetermined?

We like the machine metaphor because it gives us the illusion of control, but it is human creativity and attention to the needs and desires of others that guide the business world. Efficiency comes secondary to satisfaction, every time.

"The Information Revolution"

Today, of course, our favorite machine images and consequently our favorite metaphors tend to involve computers and software rather than the machines of the industrial age. "Input" replaces knowledge and conversation, and all plans become "programs." Every human relation becomes an "interface," and we begin to describe the workings of our own minds in the computer language of memory banks, downtime, glitches, data searches, and so on. We become, so to speak, walking examples of artificial intelligence.

Computers, of course, have special utility and fascination as management tools, although whether computerization does in fact make all industries more efficient is a matter that is still in dispute.[25] But what was once true of the old machines continues to be true (at least for the foreseeable future) of computers: They do only what we tell them to do. They are well designed, or not. They do not learn or create (although their ability to process information is, of course, staggering). They do not have insights. And, of course, they don't complain. They don't get bored. They don't have frustrated ambitions. They don't get hurt. They don't have to be talked to or, worse, listened to, much less with sympathy. They are easily (and often) replaced. They are, however sophisticated, mere machines, and a dangerous model for human thinking.

Nonaka and Takeuchi, in *The Knowledge Creating Company*, make the good point that tacit knowledge, knowledge attained only by experience, is as essential to business success as explicit knowledge, which is more of a product than a presupposition or a mere tool.[26] Adjustment and adaptation to new circumstances is beyond the range of most machines. The inner workings of most corporations (and of the business world as such) are far more flexible and organic than the machine metaphor would suggest (and, indeed, such organic metaphors replaced most mechanism metaphors in the past century). Or, to put the matter in another way, information is no longer the solution to our management problems; it has itself become the problem. We are overwhelmed with information. What we need is *knowledge* and, more important, *wisdom*, not more information. That requires interpretation of the data, a peculiarly human enterprise, and it requires purposive practices in which all of that information is sifted through and sorted and put to good use. Lack of information can be a disaster for a company, but these days, the more probable disasters are the lack of coordination of information, the lack of communication of information, the lack of an adequate sense of the purpose of the information.

The problem with computer metaphors is that special abilities of human beings—to forge projects and purposes, to work together to establish ways of working together to optimize everyone's individual skills and talents, to enjoy and be motivated by what others are doing—get lost in the fascination with mere information processing. What gets lost from view is the importance of experience, cooperation, and community. Whatever the state of the ongoing "revolution," computers are tools for people, not the other way around. People do not just serve purposes; they first of all have purposes and personalities of their own.

"The Game of Business"

Wars are brutal and jungles are uncivilized. Machines are inhuman, and, besides, has everyone forgotten that work and business can be rewarding and enjoyable? Geofferey James points out that the "Electronic Elite," as he calls the top high-tech companies, have succeeded in part because they have made the work fun—working even sixty-, seventy-, ninety-hour weeks.[27] Business competition leads quite naturally to an emphasis on winning, but we've gotten more civilized in our competitive imagery and now realize (how did we ever not realize?) that people don't function mechanically. To think that people are therefore irrational is to endorse a dangerous notion of rationality, rationality as mere efficiency. What is missing is the idea that people actually enjoy doing what they do, over and above the achievement of purposes. They are motivated not just by goals but by the activity itself.

The game metaphor came to the fore in the 1960s (when life itself was commonly viewed as a game). Business was no longer described so bloodthirstily as a life-and-death endeavor but as something voluntary, thrilling, challenging. Thus the sports and team imagery of much recent business talk is akin in some senses to military metaphors but without the violence and with more awareness of underlying mutual interests and rules of fair play.

Here's a new angle on the annual executive compensation debate: Too often, the justification for eight-figure CEO salaries appeals only to dubious market forces or the supposedly spectacular and irreplaceable talents of these top executives. Maybe. Maybe not. Mutual back-scratching between the CEOs and their boards is also mentioned. On the other hand, comparison is often made with leading sports celebrities, who earn as much, and more, for merely "playing." But maybe this isn't like a comparison of apples and oranges. Perhaps we would get a better understanding of the dramatic inequities in the corporate world if we were to see "winning" CEOs as sports stars of a sort. The money isn't compensation so much as it is the prize in what Robert Frank has called "the winner-take-all society."[28]

The rather benign imagery of winning the game has readily gained purchase in our sports-loving society. To be sure, business is not just a game, but, on reflection, business competition looks a lot like some familiar games and lends itself readily to sports analogies (hitting a home run, doing an end run).

In economics, the model of head-on competition naturally lends itself to precise mathematical formulation. Game theory was first conceived by John von Neumann in the early years of World War II. It was immediately seized upon by economists as a mathematical model for economic activity.[29] Even as originally conceived, game theory was not restricted to games as such. It applied to virtually all situations in which individual interests were causally and strategically interconnected, including public issues of governance, welfare, private competitions, and exchanges.

With the expansion of the theory as "decision theory," "social choice theory," and "rationality modeling," game theoretic models of competition and cooperation came to be applied to such various social and political issues as voting behavior, theories of justice, and nuclear deterrence, to name but a few. But nowhere have game theory and its applications been more enthusiastically endorsed than in economics and general business theory.

On the one hand, we are tempted to say, "How delightful! Business has now been humanized, and humanized in a recreational way." But the game metaphor is not entirely benign, and it, too, has serious drawbacks.

The main problem is that the game metaphor makes business too self-enclosed and merely coincidentally connected with productivity, service, and prosperity. (Getting a ball through a hoop has no intrinsic value. It counts only because it is part of a certain game.) Even if playing the game well gets its due emphasis, the focus is nevertheless on the play and the outcome, not on the products and not on the customer. Business tends to become a game when it loses its essential aim. It is when one thinks of business in terms of such narrow impersonal goals as making money that one loses sight of the larger enterprise. To say the obvious, most people in business don't see it as a game at all but rather as a way of making a living, a way of taking their place in society, of making a contribution.

Games also tend to be circumscribed in a way that business is not. In football, there is a clear distinction between the players and the spectators. This is precisely what is not so clear in business. In a business society, like it or not, we are all players. There is too much at stake for too many people to think of business as merely a game.

In finance, in particular, transactions too easily seem like games because of the level of abstraction of the activity. (This is what Aristotle tried to capture when he called commerce "unnatural," that is, it is cut off from the other concerns of society.) It takes some imagination and attention to appreciate the effects of market speculation and fiscal policies on flesh-and-blood people. Insofar as finance merely deals with numbers, it is easy to see the figures on the market sheet as nothing more than a scorecard.

When dealing with customers, on the other hand, the illusion of impersonality quickly disappears. (This is why it is always good managerial practice to make the "backroom" people in any organization spend some time up front with customers and their problems.) Business becomes a game only when it becomes cut off from its context, when people become numbers and means become ends. One company I worked with had developed such an obsession with game playing that the customers tended to get lost from view. Last year, a similar company suffered a precipitous drop in earnings and share values, and the CEO admitted, "We got enamored with our competitive lead and took our eye off our core products."[30] That's when games become not only dangerous to society but devastating to the company itself.

Some of the most disastrous corporate policies in recent years can be blamed on the game mentality that wholly focuses executives on "winning" and blinds them to the impact they have on others outside the game, or, for that matter, even in the game and supposedly on the same side. Executives in the early 1990s who fired faithful employees for the sake of a temporary spike in the stock price were playing such a game. The Ford strategists who figured that it would be cheaper to settle the lawsuits rather than to recall and fix the ill-fated Pinto were, in effect, playing a game. Had they instead paid attention to the suffering caused by their decisions, they certainly would not have thought of it as a game and would have followed a very different course of action.

Competition and Cowboy Capitalism

> What America needs is not to be more competitive, but more cooperative.
>
> —Ed Freeman, Darden School of Business

Competition is said to be the backbone of business, the engine that makes it move, the "magic" of the market. Much of this, of course, is sheer demagoguery, one more macho metaphor—the self-gratifying male image of the lone Wild West champion taking on all comers and "proving" himself against every challenger. It is what Ed Freeman has called "cowboy capitalism," without, I hope, thereby meaning to question the integrity of those rough and underpaid herd-tenders who have enough to cope with without having to live up to a cinematic myth as well.

And yet, it is simply untrue that American business loves competition. No one would pretend that Hertz was delighted when "number two" Avis rose in the market to become a true competitor.

No one should think that IBM was thrilled by the rapid success of Apple and then Compaq and Dell and a couple dozen other computer companies that came to challenge its onetime domination of the information market. The rise of foreign competition is even more spectacular. What passed for competition between American automakers in the 1950s and 1960s was, in retrospect, a friendly game of cards in the cozy living room of an exclusive club. None of the players welcomed the new competition from Japan or the loss of market share to the Germans.

To be sure, each of these increases in competition greatly improved the industries and the companies involved. But let us be clear about the nature of the competitive spirit. Competition is extremely valuable and often necessary in business, but it is not as such the purpose or goal of business life. The problem is that competition tends to eclipse what business is really all about and, in so doing, leads to business failure.

In a recent study at the University of Pennsylvania's Wharton School, students were asked to role-play a hypothetical business negotiation. The participants most often chose to beat the competition, regardless of whether it meant more profit to them or not. "Their desire to be Number One outweighed their economic rationality."[31] Businesses that look only at the competition and think in terms of winning rather than achieving and satisfying their customers are simply looking in the wrong direction. Even in the most serious competitions, a 100-meter dash, for example, it is essential to keep your eye on the goal, not on the competition.

There is healthy competition, and there is sick, debilitating, depraved competition. There is constructive, positive, even inspiring competition, and there is mutually destructive, negative, inhibiting competition. War and jungle metaphors give us the latter, along with all zero-sum games whose point is to punch out your opponent, debilitate the competition, and win at his or her expense. Business competition, by contrast, offers us the best example of the former, in which competition serves as a spur to one's own excellence and productivity. It provides incentives to improve, creating new heroes, ideals, and possibilities.

Competition is beneficial only within a system that can distinguish healthy from unhealthy, positive from merely negative competition. Business competition in particular is possible and makes sense only within a framework of mutual interests, integrity, and cooperation. The most basic contract presupposes an ethical world of (qualified) mutual trust and dependable commitments. The most ruthless business competition assumes from the start that equality is better than mutual destruction. Even in zero-sum betting games, the win-or-lose competition presupposes a context of cooperation. And when we consider the many kinds of competition, between creative artists as well as between nations and football teams, we begin to appreciate how one-sided our usual view of head-to-head, all-or-nothing competition is. (The second-best football team in the world is the "loser" of the Superbowl. Avis was right. There is nothing wrong with being number two.)

The most insightful entrepreneurs (Henry Ford, and Steven Jobs at Apple, for example) don't enter a market that is already crowded with competitors. Rather they find or invent an entirely new one. They are moved by the excitement of their ideas, by the challenge of the project, by the promise of success, not by competition as such. Competition is, I think, greatly overrated as a spur to innovation.

There can be no doubt about the value of competition, but it is a corrective and a constraint. It is not the carrot but, perhaps, more the stick that serves as a constant warning: Nothing here is guaranteed or assured; there are no ultimate monopolies; and business (your business) exists only because it succeeds in serving a purpose, in satisfying consumers, and if it fails to do so, or someone else can do it better or with more appeal, then the stick finds its mark and measures out its punishment.

But thinking this way, "paranoid" in Andrew Grove's lexicon, is to get our motivation the wrong way around. The first car company did not begin by competing with other car companies, and the first computer company did not begin by competing with other computer companies. Their founders had a great idea, and they ran with it. The best businesses get clear about what they are doing, stay open to new opportunities, and get clear about who they are. They are most competitive when they do not compete at all. They follow their values and develop their virtues, and winning then comes as a matter of course.

The Myth of the Entrepreneur

The underlying metaphor of so much of our thinking—though again we rarely think of it as a metaphor—is our much celebrated idea of "the individual" and, in business especially, "the self-made man or woman." But even a genius has to be sufficiently steeped in the culture that makes his or her invention possible. We will never understand the world of business (or any other human world) unless we begin with human interrelations and how people "fit" into cultures, organizations, and institutions. It is not first of all individual motives and attributes that make the business world possible. It is an established set of *practices*, in which implicit rules, tacit knowledge, and collective values, needs, and understandings, not individual personalities, are the principal structure.

One business hero of particular interest, especially in light of current corporate uncertainty, is the entrepreneur.[32] The entrepreneur, according to the familiar John Wayne mythology, is the lone frontiersman who single handedly sets up an industry or perhaps establishes a whole new world.[33] The myth is thus part and parcel of a much older American myth, the myth of individualism, the myth of the solitary hero. The entrepreneur simply brings John Wayne up-to-date and puts him firmly at the center of the business world.

The continuing corporate obsession with the almost mythological character called *the entrepreneur* is both unrealistic and, if taken seriously, counterproductive. Most people are not entrepreneurial (and cheapening the word by taking any initiative or innovation as entrepreneurship only fogs our understanding about what this phenomenon really is). I have attacked the inappropriateness of such a concept within the typical corporate setting at length elsewhere,[34] but here I want to make a different kind of point, one borrowed from Fernando Flores and his colleagues.[35] Entrepreneurship is itself a social practice, and it consists, in part, of appreciating marginal or neglected aspects of more general social practices. Jobs and Wozniak, for example, did not by themselves create the world of personal computing. Rather they recognized a significant gap, an anomaly in the world of computing, communication, and office management. They did not create a world so much as they opened up the world in a new way or disclosed a new world, so to speak. This is true entrepreneurship.

It may be true that behind every successful business is some entrepreneur, that is, one of those relatively rare individuals who is both creative and business-minded, who is willing to take considerable risks and work single-mindedly to turn a dream into a marketable reality. But corporations, once formed, do not operate on the same risk-prone, creative principles that motivated the originator of the business, and the corporate world could not possibly function if, as we so often hear, everyone were to aspire to be an entrepreneur.

The truth is rather that what makes corporations work and flourish is not the rapid turnaround and enormous risk undertaken by the entrepreneur; it is precisely that dependability and security that come with knowing who you are and what you are doing. A sense of security among employees who trust the corporation's stability and fairness is at least as essential as the trust of the consumers who buy its products and services. Indeed, these often turn out to be one and the same.

The continuous efforts to "shake up" the corporation and "give it some new blood" with cruel and usually destructive mass firings result in an even more timid and slow-moving beast. Seminars on innovation and change may help to allay some fears but often distract good employees from the real challenges they face, to keep on doing what they already do conscientiously and well. What the corporate world needs is not more entrepreneurs, although America is producing them by the hundreds of thousands. On the contrary, what most corporations need to cultivate is more of those unheralded heroes who used to be called, with some disdain, "the company man" (now "the company woman," too). These are people who are content to submerge their individual identities with the organization and live their lives so that their companies can prosper. Sacrificing such people for not being sufficiently entrepreneurial is like removing one's skeleton because it is overly rigid. With all of the celebration of change, we are too prone to ignore what really endures. Stability, not innovation alone, makes companies and their people secure and successful.

Abstract Greed

Money's easy to make if it's money you want. But with a few
exceptions people don't want money. They want luxury and they
want love and they want admiration.

—John Steinbeck, *East of Eden*

In the 1987 Oliver Stone film *Wall Street*, Michael Douglas (playing
the fictional Gordon Gekko) delivered a particularly concise
formulation of what many people, in retrospect, thought was wrong
with that whole decade. "Greed is good," he proclaimed (echoing a
real-life speech by Ivan Boesky, a few years before). This vulgarization
of Adam Smith's model of free enterprise, in which self-interest had
a carefully contained and nuanced meaning, had long been familiar.
The doctrine of the "invisible hand" (converting acts of individual
greed into the blessing of universal prosperity) had worked its way
deep into the American ideology, and, accordingly, there was nothing
too extreme or too good to be said about greed. But, what is greed?
Why has it been considered a vice and a sin throughout most of
human history? Why do we still use the word *greedy* not as a term of
praise but as a criticism, a put-down, a condemnation?

Plato referred to *pleonexia*, a serious vice that might best be
understood as *grasping*. There is a fine line between idealism and
ambition, which one might describe as "reaching," and avarice and
greed, which are something quite different. "Grasping" has a sense of
desperation about it, something unseemly, the unmistakable
suggestion of "too much." And that is what greed is, "too much." In
the film *Key Largo*, Edward G. Robinson discovers in a word what he
has always wanted, what drives his vicious criminal career: "more!" he
says with gleeful enthusiasm, "that's it, *more!!*"

"Greed is good" is a contradiction. Greed is by definition *not good*.
But that, of course, doesn't answer the question: What is wrong with
greed?

Greed (avarice) is an excess. It is like gluttony, an embarrassment,
and the explanation "I wanted more" does not serve as an excuse but
rather confirms the unbridled vulgarity. Given our characterization of
business as irreducibly social and necessarily involved with mutual
interests and concerns, the supposed place of greed in business

mentality is surely embarrassing in itself. And yet, the idea that greed is basic to business has been firmly established, if not by its practitioners, then certainly by its critics. How odd, then, that we so often celebrate and reward greed as "ambition" and "drive." Greed is not vision. It is a lack of vision. Let us see it for what it is, an extreme form of selfishness, an oblivion to all virtues, and neglect or contempt for any good but one's own.

Nevertheless, the ideology of greed takes on a life of its own. A few years ago, I asked my business ethics students, rather casually, how much money they thought that they could reasonably expect to be earning ten years from then. An economics major asked how she was supposed to know about ten years of potential inflation, so I assured the class that 1997 dollars would do. A few students confessed that they had no idea what they wanted to do for a living yet, so they couldn't estimate an expected income. I told them that at the moment I was more interested in their expectations than I was in their career choices, and I asked for a few volunteers.

"Thirty-five thousand dollars," offered one student in the middle of the classroom. The rest of the class, almost as one, chortled and guffawed.

"Too high or too low?" I asked, tongue-in-cheek, the answer being obvious.

"You can't even live on thirty-five thousand dollars a year," insisted one perturbed student, "even without a family."

"Well," I needled them, "how much would it take to live on?"

"A hundred grand," shouted a student at the back of the class, and almost everyone nodded or muttered in agreement.

"And do you think that you will make that much?" I asked.

"Sure," answered the same student, with more cockiness than confidence.

"How?" I asked.

"Oh, I haven't the slightest idea. Probably in investments," he answered with a nervous giggle.

Everyone laughed. I then asked the class (there were about a hundred of them) to write down the figure they "reasonably expected" to be earning in a decade, adjusted for inflation, etc. The class average was well over seventy-five thousand dollars a year, not counting a few visionary millionaires-to-be who were not counted in the averages.[36] (The average American income was less than half that.)

I often do that experiment, and I get much the same result and discussion every time. I'm happy to say that since the beginning of the 1990s, the figures have become more modest and the ambitions more along the lines of "doing something worthwhile with my life." But whether this is because of a new social consciousness or because of economic despair and pessimism about jobs, I cannot say.

What impresses me is not so much the large and sometimes enormous sums of money these students seemed to think that they wanted, deserved, and needed to live on but their utter naiveté about how to get it and, even more, their remarkable lack of sense about what to do with it. It is the money that counted—no, not even the money but the sheer numbers themselves. Of course, there are always luxuries to covet and to buy, but there was very little desire for such things themselves, only an abstract desire for the numbers. Questions about "why," "what," and "how" would just have to wait their turn.

I have called this phenomenon *abstract greed*. It is greed without desire, greed learned but not comprehended, a brainwashed sense that this is what one ought to want. It was furthermore obvious that if most of these students actually had the desire and expectation for such an income, they would be doomed to a life of frustration and failure.

Better to listen to what the Talmud says: "The rich man is one who is satisfied with what he has." The first question to ask is, "what do we really want?" and "what do we really need?" Success in business is or ought to be indistinguishable from success in life, success as a person, success as a citizen. More is not necessarily better. To think otherwise is to embrace a vice, thinking that it is a virtue.

The Myth of the Profit Motive

Abstract greed is a falsification of what drives people, but there is an analog that is no less abstract but much more insidious in the corporate context. It is what business theorists in the twentieth century have often called the *profit motive*. Never mind that the phrase was invented by nineteenth-century socialists as an attack on business and its narrow-minded pursuit of the dollar, the mark, and the yen to the exclusion of all other considerations and obligations. The idea is that the natural desire for profit drives the free enterprise system (and so, too, each one of us).

A more sophisticated version of the myth of the profit motive avoids the extravagant generalizations regarding human nature, interpreting the motive more modestly as a matter of contractual obligation, not natural necessity. "The social responsibility of business," writes Milton Friedman in a famous polemical article, "is to increase profits."[37] He does not include the word *only*, but it is clearly implied. Friedman argues that the managers of a company have a fiduciary responsibility to the owners (in a publicly held company, the stockholders), which is certainly true. But notice that Friedman's argument, although it is headlined in terms of profits, is in fact concerned with the notion of responsibility, not a profit concept at all. Managers and executives may make profits, but not (as such) for themselves.

Such talk of the profit motive, I want to suggest, causes more damage than any amount of sleaziness or dishonest dealings on the part of the business community. It is the narrow-minded language of the profit motive that gives rise to public suspicion. Peter Drucker, in his magnum opus *Management*, writes of managers that "it is their own rhetoric that is one of the main reasons for hostility. . . . There is only the profit motive, [but] why that desire should be indulged in by society any more than bigamy, for instance, is never explained."[38]

"Profit" is an economist's term. It is not merely an increase in wealth, and it is not what one earns when one works for a living. As one of my entrepreneurial friends once said to me—before he lost a fortune on an unfortunate investment—"You'll never get rich working for a living." Profit is, technically, what is "left over" after all costs have been paid. In practice, profits are often what the board or the boss says that they are. But profits are neither "natural" nor a motive. Anthony Flew, defending profits but attacking the idea of a "profit motive," rightly asks whether we should also talk about a "wage motive," a "rent motive," and an "interest motive."[39] This little *reductio ad absurdum* quickly demolishes its target. Of course, people work for profits in a profit-making system. But profits are a means to an end—for a corporation, survival, for an individual, money to spend. Profits get distributed and reinvested. Profits are a means to building the business and rewarding employees, executives, and investors.

The profit motive is often attacked as a form of selfishness. Once again Flew makes the point rather nicely. He carefully distinguishes pursuing one's interest from selfishness, taking as an example his daughters eating their dinners: "It would be monstrous to denounce them as selfish hussies, simply on that account." Flew adds that "the time for denunciation could come only after one of them had, for instance, eaten someone else's dinner too."[40]

Who is supposed to have this so-called profit motive? Employees don't have it: They have a salary to earn and a job to do. Managers don't have it: They have obligations and responsibilities. Top executives, too, work for salaries and bonuses. They work for profits only insofar as they are also shareholders in the company. It is only the investors, the "owners," who do not "work for" profits, and if anyone has the profit motive, presumably they do. It is on their behalf, according to this myth, that the entire system functions.

But stockholders are not *homines economici*, that is, merely economic self-maximizing beings. They are people with values and virtues who presumably care about something more in life than how their shares are doing. To be sure, they do hope and often expect to make a profit. And that means that the businesses themselves have to make a profit. In Peter Drucker's startling turn of phrase: "If archangels instead of businessmen sat in directors' chairs, they would still have to be concerned with profitability, despite their total lack of personal interests in making profits."[41]

But businesses and businesspeople make a profit only by supplying quality goods and services, by providing jobs, by supplying capital and taking risks, and by fitting into the community. Norman Bowie has argued that profits, like happiness, are most easily obtained when not pursued as such. If you want to be happy, you need to pursue not happiness but other goals. So, too, "the more a business consciously seeks to obtain profits, the less likely they are to achieve them." Bowie aptly calls this "the profit-seeking paradox."[42] One might think of it as a conceptual antidote to the mythical profit motive.

The Myth of Altruism

The most insidious trap in business ethics is the forced polarity between what one ought to do and what is in one's own self-interest, as if these were always and necessarily opposed. To be sure, they are occasionally opposed, but more often than not their opposition betrays a lack of vision, thought, and imagination. The trite phrase, that businesses "do well by doing good," speaks volumes about a better way to think about these things, one that harks back to Aristotle.

Adam Smith's casual metaphor, "the invisible hand," gives a false picture of his philosophy. (He only actually used this image once in *Wealth of Nations*). He did indeed write about self-interest, but his ideas are very different from the "greed is good" caricature that is often presented in his name. In particular, Smith noticed that most of what we want most in the world, and, therefore, what is most central to our self-interest, is being thought well of by others. In business, needless to say, being thought well of is an essential precondition to any continuing relationship not based on coercion or dire necessity.

Smith insisted that what people really want is respect and approval. They want love and admiration if they can get it, but this means that our self-interest is intimately tied up with *serving the interests of others*. Thus the polarity between doing what is in our interest and doing the right thing—or doing things for other people—breaks down. In serving others, we serve ourselves. The language of "self-sacrifice" is misleading, at best. The conflict between our own interests and others' interests is rare.

When corporations struggle over the choice between self-interest (profitability) and doing right (treating the employees or customers fairly, paying attention to the surrounding community), it is almost always a symptom of unimaginative, nonstrategic, short-term thinking. Fred Reichheld, author of *The Loyalty Effect*, comments that "it is foolish to think you can ignore employees' family demands and still get committed, energetic, long-term employees. That's fairyland." Fairyland, indeed. What too many people still insist on thinking about in terms of "ethics" is and always has in fact been just plain good business. The conflict between self-interest and doing right is usually an illusion, but, like so many illusions, thinking can make it so.

Corporations often have to struggle with this illusion from the other end. It drives executives rightly batty when their good deeds are inevitably interpreted as "just so much PR," as a sneaky way to get some advertising, or as just another tax deduction. Consider the following response to a corporate ethics award in Canada last year:

> No member of the public nominated a big corporation, which probably says something about the suspicion people have about corporations. When, for example, a transnational corporation . . . donates to a foundation or a university, the public tends to think it's trying to avoid taxes. And although there is truth in that, it's not unethical for a company to pursue both self-interest and public good at the same time.[43]

Many examples bear this out. Chase Manhattan Bank gives a gift of a hundred thousand dollars or so to the Museum of Natural History in New York. One can imagine a suspicious cynic wanting to know why. Mobil Oil sponsors *Masterpiece Theater* for twenty-five years, and the charge is made that "it's only PR." Texaco sponsors the Metropolitan Opera on radio for decades—for most people, their only opportunity to hear fine opera. The critics quickly hone in: What are they trying to cover up? Milton Friedman adds to the confusion with his famous charge that such charitable giving (on the part of corporations, not individuals) is nothing less than theft (from the stockholders), an insidious form of socialism. But does it have to be proven to the myopic stockholder who can see only his share price and dividends that such community-minded activities do indeed improve profitability? (Could one ever conclusively prove this?) Why assume that doing good is appropriate only insofar as it does not also serve financial self-interest? Doesn't this undermine the whole idea of free enterprise? And aren't we putting ourselves in the odd position where two rights come out to make a wrong?

An Aristotelian focus on the virtues and integrity makes one fundamental point: Being virtuous is by its very nature *both* acting in one's own self-interest and acting in a way that is socially productive. The question "who really benefits?" is a misunderstanding. To transcend the opposition of self-interest (profitability) and ethics is what the focus on the virtues is all about. Whether or not virtue is "its own reward," the virtues on which one prides oneself in personal life are essentially the same as those essential to good business—honesty, dependability, courage, loyalty, and, in short, integrity. To be virtuous, in other words, is to act in one's own *best* interests.

PART II

A Better Way to Think About Business
The Meaning of Integrity

> A superior person thinks of what is right.
> An inferior person thinks only of what is profitable.
> —Confucius

The Virtues of Free Enterprise

In the nineteenth century, it was common wisdom that business had become the great civilizing influence in Europe. Some writers may have rightly feared for a loss of culture, but in place of sectarian massacres in the name of religion and hundred-year feuds in the pursuit of a throne or some parcel of land, the new world of business offered compromise, mutual gain, innovation, and widespread wealth on a scale never before imagined. Napoleon was replaced by thousands of entrepreneurs, merchants, and bankers. A decade of war (1805–1815) slipped quietly into a century of peace and prosperity.

It is generally supposed that the great economist Adam Smith promised that general prosperity would follow from the iron laws of free enterprise, notably the law of supply and demand and the pursuit of self-interest. In fact, Smith and everyone else knew that free enterprise would be possible only if business and businesspeople perceived themselves in terms of something more than the mere pursuit of profits, as the civilizing force that they were, in terms of a good life well lived as well as a comfortable life rich in material possessions and economic power. Not surprisingly, a turn-of-the-century theorist of capitalism, Max Weber, famously linked the new enterprise to the spirit of modern religion.

True, there is much to dismay us about commercialism. Weber expressed his concerns about the loss of spirituality, and Adam Smith had already expressed his doubts about the dangers of monopoly and the motives of some businessmen. In many parts of the world, free enterprise has not proved its promise of prosperity for all, and the gap between rich and poor, the haves and the have-nots, continues to grow. But what we too easily tend to forget—or just plain take for granted—is the big picture. Business has been and remains a civilizing influence. At the very heart of business is the need to be aware of and concerned with other people's interests and desires, and to go about efficiently trying to satisfy them. At the very heart of business are the skills of negotiation and compromise. And at the very heart of business is the recognition of the necessity of trust, the importance of a good reputation and a good name in the community.

In one of the most famous passages in *Wealth of Nations*, Adam Smith declares, "It is not from the benevolence of the butcher, the brewer, or the baker that we expect our dinner, but from regard to their own self-interest. We address ourselves, not to their humanity but to their self-love, and never talk to them of our own necessities but of their advantages." This is often quoted in defense of self-interest, sometimes accompanied with a sneering contempt for mere altruism. But what is usually missed is the obvious. The self-interest of the butcher, the brewer, and the baker is served only because they do indeed pay attention to our necessities, as well as to their own reputations for quality and fairness. It is essential to their business that they do so. It is precisely because they rise above their own self-interests and consider the interests of others that they make a success of their enterprise. What they ultimately "sell" is their own integrity.

The usual justification of capitalism is the prosperity that it supposedly ensures. Andrew Carnegie, writing in 1889, pointed out:

> the poor enjoy what the rich could not before afford. What were the luxuries have now become the necessities of life. The laborer has now more comforts than the farmer had a few generations ago. The farmer has more luxuries than the landlord had, and is more richly clad and better housed. The landlord has books and pictures rarer, and appointments more artistic, than the King could then obtain.

One might question some of Carnegie's generalities, and one would certainly challenge his defense of today's enormous inequalities between rich and poor. But we should take seriously the claim that the goal of the free enterprise system is general prosperity, and business at its best is philanthropy ("love of people") writ large. Self-congratulatory as that might seem, it also lifts business out of the mire of mere self-interest and points to a very different aspect of free enterprise, namely the virtues it requires. To be sure, there are always exceptions—every practice has its cheats and creeps, but the underlying virtues of business, without any self-serving ideological nonsense, are to be civilized and civilizing.

Even a casual observation of the general goodwill and genuine amiability of most businesspeople tells us something very important about the business world. Free enterprise celebrates our different talents, tastes, and peculiarities, whatever they may be. Strangers and outsiders, for example, have been the focus of suspicion throughout history. In business, by contrast, strangers and foreigners are potential customers.

All too often, business talk and business thinking do not reflect this basic idea, that business life is first of all a matter of civility, of integrity, of cultivating the virtues. And the virtues include not only the obvious entrepreneurial virtues of thrift, tough-mindedness, and cleverness but the civic and civil virtues of caring (e.g., for customers, for employees, and for the community), of cooperation and trust (among competitors as well as allies), of fairness and loyalty (to one's friends, one's family, one's company, one's community). When business is cut off from the rest of human enterprise, in such slogans as "business is business," for example, cynics suggest what is simply not true. Business is not "just business." It is not self-contained, with its own rationale, its own rules, its own reason for being. It is, essentially, a part of human life and human community.

The sheer size of modern enterprise does little to help our thinking. Our sense of ethics developed in small communities—families, neighborhoods, classrooms, and congregations. Multinational corporations worth billions of dollars with millions of stockholders and hundreds of thousands of employees strain our thinking. The sad consequence is that we have developed this impersonal image of "The Corporation" along with the law's idea that a corporation is a "legal fiction," designed for the sole purpose of limiting liability and producing profits. The contemporary manager, working for executives that he or she may never meet and for stockholders who are never seen, fearing for his or her future and burdened by an avalanche of impersonal paper, quite naturally comes to think of the job as a compromise between one's real self, on the one hand, and the impersonal pressures of the position, on the other. The human virtues, if they are not squeezed out of the picture altogether, too easily come to be viewed as irrelevant to the job and to business. What gets lost is an adequate sense of integrity.

The Meaning of Integrity

An honest man . . . the noblest work of God.
—Alexander Pope (Essay on Man)

Integrity is not itself a virtue so much as it is a synthesis of the virtues, working together to form a coherent whole. This is what we call, in the moral sense, *character*. The word *integrity* means "wholeness," wholeness of virtue, wholeness as a person, wholeness in the sense of being an integral part of something larger than the person—the community, the corporation, society, humanity, the cosmos. Integrity thus suggests a holistic view of ourselves, although the word *holism* has suffered considerably from New Age excess and has accumulated a consequent aura of fuzziness. Unfortunately, too, the word *integrity*, like *honor* (its close kin), has suffered considerable abuse in recent years, particularly in politics. In the current climate of cynicism, both terms have come to seem all but archaic, overly idealistic, unrealistic.

This is a misunderstanding. Far from being an exceptional virtue, peculiar to saints, integrity is essential to a decent life. It is what endures through change and trauma. It is, in the recent vernacular, simply "getting it all together," seeing one's life as a whole, as a coherent and virtuous character. Integrity, in fact, is surprisingly common, however many well-publicized exceptions we see. It is an illusion to think that a busy life in business could be entirely conflict-and trouble-free, of course, but integrity is that sense of cohesion such that one is not torn apart by conflicts. Integrity is not a magical preventative, an inoculation against ethical dilemmas. But a sense of one's own integrity is what allows us to navigate the treacherous waters of those dilemmas, and though integrity does not guarantee success, there can be no success without it.

To some managers, integrity suggests stubbornness and inflexibility, a refusal to be a "team player." But to reject integrity and the importance of character, to find fault with an employee who insists on "drawing the line," for example, is self-destructive. For every employee who is a "troublemaker," there will be fifty who are effective and loyal, but, nevertheless, they will all insist on drawing the line somewhere. Those employees prevent many a company from taking a dangerous or disastrous step over the line. Good management is not silencing or discouraging ethical employees but listening to them. Listening (attentiveness), in fact, is one of the essential virtues for integrity.

Integrity is often understood as honesty. But honesty is more limited than integrity, and there may be times when integrity requires being less than candid, even untruthful. Stephen L. Carter tells the story of a man who, lying on his deathbed, "confesses" to his grieving wife that he had an affair, years before.[44] In an obvious sense, this is an instance of honesty (he is telling the truth), but is it an example of integrity? Carter comes down firmly, and we surely agree, that this cleansing of conscience was cruel and unnecessary, without consideration for his spouse, and the very antithesis of integrity. Integrity is looking at the larger picture, in which the well-being of his surviving wife must be central. His honesty serves no purpose but a selfish one. Integrity, whatever else it may be, is not inconsiderate selfishness.

Integrity is sometimes understood as resisting temptation, but this is an overly negative vision. Integrity more often requires action and pro active behavior; it is not just "not giving in." A person who errs may have much more integrity than a person who simply abstains. A person in business who maintains his or her integrity by doing nothing does not understand what integrity in business is.

Integrity is often understood as resisting or refusing the orders of others, but, more often, integrity requires obedience and loyalty. Integrity as "wholeness" has just as much to do with one's coherent connections and relationships with other people and institutions as it does with one's relation to oneself. Properly fulfilling one's role or position is as essential to integrity as a clean conscience. Again, simply not doing wrong is not enough to do right. The key, of course, is that those others or those institutions, one's role and one's position, must be compatible with one's own values and virtues, and vice versa. When an individual willingly joins an organization (a corporation), agrees to act on its behalf and in its interests, and agrees with its aims and values, obedience and loyalty are part and parcel of integrity.

When one comes to disagree with those aims and values, integrity may require disobedience and disloyalty, perhaps resignation. But this makes it seem as if integrity has two very different meanings, one of them encouraging conformity and obedience, the other urging a belligerent independence.[45] But this is misleading. Integrity includes both one's sense of membership and loyalty and one's sense of moral autonomy. "Wholeness" means that one's identity is not that of an isolated atom but rather the product of a larger social molecule, and that wholeness includes—rather than excludes—other people and one's social roles.

A person's integrity on the job typically requires him or her to follow the rules and practices that define that job. And yet, critical encounters sometimes require a show of integrity that is indeed antithetical to one's assigned role and duties. Here again we get confused by the highlighting of an exceptional case of conflict when the paradigm is rather the synthesis of one's own values and the values of the organization. To be sure, there are conflicts—for example, your boss tells you to "cook" the books and you know that it is wrong, but on reflection it becomes evident that the conflict is not between two norms of integrity, but between your own integrity and your boss's lack of it.

The contrary of integrity—lack of integrity—can take on many forms. Integrity is not something a person "has," and it is not a particular act or activity that one does (or does not do). Whereas a single action may betray the lack of integrity, there is no single action (or, indeed, any number of actions) that will definitively establish a person's integrity. This is, perhaps, why integrity is so heavily guarded, and why people will go to such lengths to deny their own misdeeds and corruption. A single slip can be fatal, whereas a lifetime of good deeds still leaves open the question of one's ultimate righteousness.[46]

Without Integrity: The Hypocrite, the Opportunist, and the Chameleon

Here is one version of a classic joke: "Integrity. If you can fake that, you've got it made." The joke is that integrity cannot be faked. It is, by its very nature, the real thing. The uncompromising nature of integrity explains why it is that a single flaw or failing typically leads to others, indeed, to a system of rationalizations and cover-ups that betray a lack of integrity more demonstrably than the original misdeed. For example, *hypocrisy* stands at direct odds with integrity. A hypocrite fails to practice what he preaches, but the lack of integrity is most obvious in the fragmentation of the self, the break in wholeness, that is required by saying one thing and doing another. It is not simply a breach between action and language, but an enormously complex form of self-deception. The action in question is redescribed in language that slips around the stated prohibition ("I wasn't really stealing it; I was just borrowing it for a while" or "That was no bribe; that was a token of my appreciation for services already rendered").

Two familiar examples of the lack of integrity in the corporate setting are the opportunist and the chameleon.[47] What is striking about these two modes of corruption is the fact that neither of them need involve dishonesty or hypocrisy (although, like many vices, they often welcome such company). Neither do they involve any obvious inconsistency, at least from the person's own point of view. An opportunist does not usually have any principles that we would readily recognize as ethical, and therefore there may be no standard to which he or she can be faithful.

But isn't such a person being "true to self"? This is why it is essential that our "public" and our personal sense of integrity fit together as unity, for consistency requires something more than fidelity to a single, selfish goal. It also involves coherence and respect for other people. It requires fidelity to self in the midst of others and together with them. The opportunist merely uses others as his or her instruments. But if integrity is being "true to oneself," it does indeed follow (as Polonius preaches) that you will be true to others as well. Integrity is the very contrary of using other people to one's own ends, but it is also being clear about what our true ends are.

The chameleon displays a similar lack of integrity in his or her total absence of not only principles but goals as well, unless we want to accept "fit in and do whatever seems to please other people" as some sort of purpose in life. The chameleon is a lizard, of course, that has the remarkable ability to change its colors depending on the context, and the typical corporate yes-man is like a lizard, crawling from executive to executive and changing colors accordingly. (Luckily for the lizard, the colors within a corporation often tend to be more or less uniform.) But when questions of method and purpose are opened up and equally powerful voices disagree, the chameleon is in trouble—something like finding itself on a background of plaid. Thus the fragile consistency of the chameleon, whose tenuous appearance of integrity depends on the uniformity of other people, fractures into incoherence. This is how one distinguishes the vices of the chameleon from the virtue of loyalty, of course; loyalty is stalwart and (within reason) unshifting. The chameleon has no integrity because he or she has no self, only a reflection of the social situation.

At the other extreme is a special form of hypocrisy that is so widely confused with real integrity that it deserves special mention. It is to be found particularly in those who loudly proclaim their own integrity. The "Person of Integrity" wears integrity as a self-conscious badge to be worn in public (and no doubt in the privacy of the shower as well), and any and every challenge to his or her opinions (on whatever subject) is considered a moral challenge (reflecting a lack of integrity in the challenger). The Person of Integrity proclaims principles, to which he or she may be ruthlessly obedient, but the odd thing about principles is the fact that the more general they are, the more they admit interpretations and exceptions. And so, not surprisingly, whatever is in his or her best interest turns out to be the "right" thing to do backed by absolute principle. And so the Person of Integrity is impossible to argue with, dangerous to disagree with, and as unpredictable as the opportunist or the chameleon. Whereas the opportunist and the chameleon shift with the winds and the situation, the Person of Integrity pretends to be the moral rock around which the rest of the earth revolves while nevertheless serving only his or her own demands.

Integrity requires willingness to negotiate and to compromise as well as conviction and commitment. The idea that integrity means being closed to outside influences and temptations as opposed to open to others is a grotesque and dangerous misunderstanding. Whatever else integrity means to us today, it involves getting along with other people, subject only to some rather extreme moral constraints (the usual "living in Nazi Germany" examples). Integrity involves openness and affection and flexibility, and, not surprisingly, an organization or corporation that has integrity will be one that is composed of open-minded, independent, but cooperative and caring individuals, not rigid, self-righteous clones. Integrity involves principles and policies, to be sure, but it also involves a pervasive sense of social context. Otherwise, it becomes mere self-righteousness, not virtue at all.

Integrity is essential to happiness. This is not to say that there are not occasions in which maintaining one's integrity causes misery, but we have to get away from that *either/or* paradigm that keeps telling us that either we are ethical and true to ourselves or we pursue our own advantage. Of course, a sufficiently corrupt person can feel happy despite a trail of evil deeds, but this, we should insist, is not happiness. Aristotle's central ethical concept of an all-embracing "happiness" tells us that doing what one ought to do, fulfilling one's responsibilities and obligations is not counter but conducive to the good life, to becoming the sort of person one wants to become. Conversely, becoming the sort of person one wants to become— which presumably includes, to a very large extent, what one does "for a living"—is what happiness is all about.

Revisioning the Corporation: The Company as Community

The Aristotelian approach begins with the idea that we are, first of all, members of communities, with shared histories and established practices governing everything from eating and working to worshipping. We are not, as our favorite folklore would have it, first of all, individuals, that is, autonomous, self-sustaining, self-defining creatures who, ideally, think entirely for ourselves and determine what we are. The "self-made" man or woman is a social creature, and he or she "makes it" by being an essential part of society, however innovative or eccentric he or she may be. To say that we are communal creatures is to say that we have mutual interests, that even in the most competitive community, our self-interests are parasitic on and largely defined in terms of those vital interests we hold in common. To think of the corporation as a community is to insist that it cannot be, no matter how vicious its internal politics, a mere collection of self-interested individuals, merely contractually related. Those who encourage such a view are, in effect, undermining the very viability of the corporation.

To be sure, communities in the contemporary world are anything but homogeneous or harmonious. The claim I am making, however, is more metaphysical than nostalgic: that is, that what we call "the individual" is socially constituted and socially situated. "The individual" today is the product of a particularly mobile and entrepreneurial society in which natural groups (notably the extended family or tribe) have been replaced by artificial organizations such as schools and corporations. Movement between them is not only possible (as it is usually not between tribes and families) but encouraged, even required. Human beings are not, as such, individuals. They are separated by the boundaries of their epidermises, to be sure, and there is a sense in which each one has his or her own thoughts and emotions. But even these are prompted by, learned from, shared with, and similar to the thoughts and emotions of other people.

"The individual" was an invention of the eleventh and twelfth centuries in Europe, when families were separated by war, and the tightly arranged structures of feudalism were breaking apart. "The individual" became increasingly important with the advent of capitalist and consumer society, but (as so often in the overly materialist history of economics) he or she became important first because of changing religious conceptions, with increased emphasis on personal faith and individual salvation. Nevertheless, "the individual" was always a relative, context-dependent designation. An individual in one society is a sociopath in another. ("The nail that sticks out is the one that gets hammered," goes a traditional Japanese proverb.)

What we call "the individual" is, from even the slightest outside perspective, very much a social, even a conformist conception. To show one's individuality in the financial world, for example, it may be imperative to wear the same tie as everyone else, usually of a color (red, yellow, pink) or a pattern (paisley) that only a true eccentric would have chosen on his own. To further emphasize individuality (which connotes creativity, even genius), one might sport a moustache or a beard (though the range of styles is very strictly circumscribed). But getting beyond trivial appearances, even our thoughts and feelings are, it is obvious, for the most part defined and delineated by our society, in our conversations and confrontations with other people.

Princeton anthropologist Clifford Geertz once wrote that a human being all alone in nature would not be a noble, autonomous being but a pathetic, quivering creature with no identity and few defenses or means of support. Our heroic conception of "the individual"—often exemplified by the lone (usually male) hero—is a bit of bad but self serving anthropology. There are exceptional individuals, to be sure, but they are social creations and become exceptional just because they serve the needs of their society, more often than not by exemplifying precisely those forms of excellence most essential to that society.

We find our identities and our meanings only within communities, and for most of us that means at work in a company or an institution. However we might prefer to think of ourselves, however much we (rightly) insist on the importance of family and friends, however much we might complain about our particular jobs or professional paths—we define ourselves largely in terms of them, even if, in desperation, in opposition to them. Whether a person likes or hates his or her job will almost always turn on relationships with the people he or she works for and works with, whether there is mutual respect or animosity and callousness or indifference. Even the lone entrepreneur—the sidewalk jeweler or the financial wizard—will succeed only if he or she has social skills and enjoys (or seems to enjoy) his or her customers or clients.

For millions of employees and managers, the corporation becomes their primary community. Even the family lives within the embrace of the corporation, and for better or worse, that institution will define the values and the conflicts of values within which one lives much of one's life. A corporation that encourages mutual cooperation and encourages individual excellence as an essential part of teamwork is a very different place to work and live than a corporation that incites "either/or" competition, antagonism, and continuous jostling for status and recognition.

The Corporation as Citizen

A corporation is also a "citizen." Whatever the legalities may be, a corporation is a member of the larger community, which is inconceivable without it. The classic arguments for "the social responsibility of business" all too readily begin with the assumption that the corporation is an autonomous, independent entity that needs to consider its obligations to the surrounding community. But corporations, like individuals, are part and parcel of the communities in which they live and flourish, and the responsibilities that they bear are not the products of philosophical argument or implicit contracts but intrinsic to their very existence as social entities.

These claims are closely akin to the ideas captured in the punlike notion of a "stakeholder," that now-familiar broadening conception of the corporate constituency that includes a variety of affected (and effective) groups and all sorts of different obligations and responsibilities. The term *stakeholder* has become something of a cover-all term, and so what considerable advantages it has provided in terms of breadth are to some extent now compromised by the uncritical overuse of the word. For example, the notion of "stakeholder" suggests discrete groups or entities, whereas the primary source of dilemmas in business ethics is the fact that virtually all of us wear (at least) two hats—for example, as employees and as members of the larger community, as consumers and as stockholders, as a manager and as a friend—and these roles can come into conflict with one another.

If we consider corporations as citizens and as communities—not as legal fictions, monolithic entities, faceless bureaucracies, and matrices of price/earnings ratios, net assets, and liabilities—then the activities and the ethics of business become much more comprehensible and much more human. Shareholders are, of course, part of the community, but most of them only marginally rather than, as in some now-classic arguments, as the sole recipients of managerial fiduciary obligations. The concept of "community" also shifts our conception of what makes a corporation work or not. What makes a corporation efficient or inefficient is not a series of well-oiled mechanical operations but the congenial interrelationships, the coordination and rivalries, team spirit and morale of the many people who work there and are in turn shaped and defined by the corporation.

So, too, what drives a corporation is not some mysterious abstraction called "the profit motive" (which is highly implausible even as a personal motive, but utter nonsense when applied to a fictitious legal entity or a bureaucracy). It is the collective will and ambitions of its employees, few of whom (even in profit-sharing plans or in employee-owned companies) work for a profit in any obvious sense. What the employees of a corporation do, they do to fit in, to do their jobs, to earn the respect of others, and to gain self-respect. They want to prove their value in their jobs, they try to show their independence or their resentment, they try to please (or intentionally aggravate) their superiors, they want to impress (or intimidate) their subordinates, they want to feel good about themselves, or they try to make the best of a bad situation. In short, any study of job satisfaction that does not pay primary attention to human relationships and questions of mutual esteem is missing the main part of the story. To understand how corporations work (and don't work) is to understand the social psychology and sociology of communities, not the logic of flowcharts or the workings of a cumbersome machine.

The defense of mergers and acquisitions is usually the need to be competitive, to reduce combined operational costs, to eliminate bad management, and, of course, "to look after the stockholders." But what has still received far too little attention in the debate over the public interest of mergers and takeovers is the utter disaster precipitated by the disruption of corporate communities, and this is over and above the palpable human disaster of putting so many people out of work. It is no surprise that a good many of the new entities created (or liberated) by takeover activity fail, and not just because of the mountain of debt typically accumulated in the process. What workforce can keep its morale in the face of the continuous threat of layoffs? What manager can function either as an authority or as a team player when his or her authority is clearly contingent and it is not even clear what "team" he or she is playing for? Such circumstances may encourage the appearance of hard work (and a great deal of *derriere* covering), but it cannot possibly encourage dedication or loyalty or any sense of enduring membership. But "membership" is what corporations are all about. To think of a corporate position as a job is already to undermine the organization. By ignoring such intangible features of business life as company morale in favor of the more easily measurable quantities listed in the financial pages, we are destroying the corporation as a community and, consequently, as a fully functional human institution.

The Virtues of a Corporate Culture

It is a sign of considerable progress that one of the dominant models of today's corporate thinking is the idea of a "corporate culture." As with any analogy or metaphor, there are, of course, disanalogies, and the concept of corporations as cultures too quickly attained the status of a fad—thus marking it for easy ridicule and imminent obsolescence. But some fads nevertheless contain important insights, and while those who insist on keeping up with the latest fashion may move on, the virtues of some recent fads may not yet have been fully appreciated.

Mark Paskin, for instance, argues that "corporations should have weak cultures and strong ethics."[48] "The lesson is clear," he writes "Forget culture and think about fair agreements."[49] He argues that cultures are intrinsically "conservative," and strong cultures "put basic beliefs, attitudes and ways of doing things beyond question." Cultures may be hard to change, but this, I want to argue, is precisely their strength. Some things should not change, notably, such virtues as trustworthiness and fairness and that sense of "belonging" that promotes loyalty. It does not follow that innovation and flexibility cannot be an essential part of a corporate culture. Fair agreements are—or are not—part of a corporate culture.

The concept of a corporate culture, first and foremost, is distinctively and irreducibly social. It presupposes the existence of an established community and it explicitly rejects atomistic individualism. Individuals are part of a culture only insofar as they play a part in that culture, participate in its development, and fit into its structure. Cultures are by their very nature (more or less) harmonious, that is, they are not possible unless people cooperate and share some minimal outlook on life. When we talk about "competitive cultures," we leave implicit the foundation of shared values and understandings that must, of necessity, underlie that competitiveness. (Thus the very strong camaraderie that typifies most such institutions, professional wrestling not excepted.)

Cultures require traditions and evolve over time. Thus the irony in the joke (real enough, ten years ago) about the CEO who brings in an anthropologist, with the instruction, "Build me a culture." Building a corporate culture, like building any serious relationship, takes time. There may be "love at first sight"—that is, an almost instantaneous attraction between a corporation and a new employee or customer— but acculturation, like love, is a process, a process of repetition and renewal, a process of discovery and incremental commitment. Thus culture gives a corporation stability, and it gives both those within it and those who have to deal with it (e.g., customers) a sense of security and familiarity.

Cultures, accordingly, have rules and rituals, which may be as superficial as particular modes of dress and grooming or as deep as the fundamental values and beliefs. These may or may not be explicitly summarized in a corporate code or mission statement, or they might just be "the way we do things around here." Every culture has an ethics. Indeed, one might argue that the culture *is* the ethics, which includes those basic rules that hold the organization together and protect it, even from itself. It is ultimately values, not people or products, that define a corporation and its culture. This may become extremely important in the midst of corporate upheaval and many cultural changes. A once mellow and laid-back organization may be forced into a competitive frenzy, but it is the basic values of the culture that keep a good corporation from degenerating into a crude dog-eat-dog environment.

These values are not abstractions, mere words on a piece of paper. They are necessarily embodied in executives, managers, and employees. Values, like the culture in general, must be lived. What everyone says is not nearly so important as what everyone does. And what they do is not mainly a matter of following rules (although that may be unavoidable for new members of the corporate community). It is a matter of making those values and the culture one's own, one's second nature, quite literally. In other words, the virtues of a culture manifest themselves in the virtues of each and (hopefully) every member of the corporation.

It is particularly important to appreciate the significance of the "culture" metaphor against the backdrop of the more vulgar, sometimes brutal, and either atomistic or mechanical metaphors we discussed in Part I. Business, in general, has been saddled (and has saddled itself) with unflattering and destructive images, thus misunderstanding itself. Corporations—both in general and as individual entities—have also tended to present themselves, despite all of their public relations work and advertising to the contrary, as juggernauts, as mechanical monsters, as faceless as the glass-and-steel buildings that typically house their headquarters. Consumers become so many numbers, and employees are reduced to so many replaceable parts. Even top management is only part of the mechanism. It is no wonder that most Americans who do not work for corporations think of them as inhuman and as inhumane places to work, and those millions who do work in and for corporations find themselves at a serious conceptual disadvantage. A culture carries right at its heart a sense of mutual belonging and the sense that one's own interests lie, not contingently but necessarily, with the group. The more we dehumanize the corporation and focus on financial rather than cultural issues, the more inefficient we will be.

So long as the corporation is viewed merely as a legal fiction created exclusively for the protection of its owners and their pursuit of profits, then to be sure all questions of values will have an aura of ephemeral mystery around them. In place of values, there will be only fiduciary obigations, defined by contract. Overemphasis on change and the sacrifice of stability—as evidenced in so many corporate shake-ups and restructurings today—will weaken the company and make it a far less efficient competitor. However "leaner" (and often "meaner") it may be, this "new" corporation is likely to be far more embroiled in internal politics and the personnel problems of coping with insecurity and anxiety than facing the competition or improving its products. The essential continuity is provided by the corporate culture.

Once we appreciate the importance of viewing the corporation as first of all a community (within a larger community) and as a culture with shared values and larger social concerns, then such questions as "Where do corporate values come from?" and "How can corporations be socially responsible?" simply disappear from view. It was only from a peculiarly narrow, overly legal, and inhumanly restricted understanding of organizations and institutions that such questions could make sense in the first place.

Corporate Codes of Ethics: What Are They For?

The values inherent in a corporate culture can be formalized and spelled out in what has come to be known as "the corporate code of ethics." In one sense, only the name is new, for virtually every company had some statement of aims, values, and policies long before ethics became a center of focus in the business world. But the idea that values are important not only to a company's identity but also to its way of doing business is an idea that has been remarkably slow in coming, and the impetus to formulate these values in the form of a code only started to become commonplace after the Watergate scandals of the early 1970s.

Sometimes, and at its best, the publication and distribution of a corporate code is an explicit expression of a set of values that has in fact governed the company and its employees for quite some time. Sometimes, and at its worst, the publication and distribution of a corporate code of ethics is a desperate attempt to persuade or threaten employees into compliance with a set of principles that does not play a significant role in the day-to-day behavior of its employees. And sometimes the code as stated is nothing but a hypocritical attempt at public relations.

Corporate codes can be short and very general, or they may be very specific and detailed about particular kinds of behavior. At its most general, a corporate code may simply assert the company's commitment to quality in its products and integrity in its dealings with the public, or it may simply remind everyone from salesperson to CEO that "the customer always comes first." Such assertions may indeed be valuable as a constant reminder of the purpose or mission of the company and act as a moral glue to hold the different parts of a complex company together. The best codes, however, take some care to spell out specific prohibitions and obligations, for example, the limitation on gifts that may be accepted by any employee or manager. Such detailed information in the company code serves as something more than a mere reminder. It gives employees and managers concrete and extremely useful advice in situations that may otherwise be extremely uncomfortable and ambiguous.

An inexperienced employee who is on a team assigned to decide between contractors for a minor yet substantial office addition is given a pair of very expensive football or opera tickets by one of the applicants for the contract. Should he or she accept these with thanks, or turn them down? A specific rule, "No employee shall accept gifts with a value of more than fifty dollars," answers the question. Of course, there will always be borderline or "gray" areas, for example, if the tickets cost $25.50 apiece. But the serious infractions do not happen on the borderline, and the occasional differences in judgment between those who insist on the "letter" of the code and those who adhere to its "spirit" are not likely to cause serious disruption in the company.

But in addition to providing such concrete guidance, such explicit prohibitions serve another, equally important function. Our inexperienced employee might find it quite difficult to rebuff the offer of a smooth-talking, experienced salesperson. How does one say "no" gracefully, when being so cajoled and pressured? But by pointing to the code of ethics, our inexperienced employee can easily explain his position and readily make his appeal to a higher authority, namely the policies of the company. In other words, the point of a code of ethics is not just to inform and prompt those who work for the company but to provide them with an instrument that will actually help them adhere to the values of the company.

There is another way of looking at codes of ethics, however, indeed, one which may even be an argument against them. Several years ago, the top management at SONY in the United States felt the need to develop a code, much as most of their American competitors had already done. The word came back from Mr. Morita, then the CEO of SONY, that such a code would be insulting to the workers. "They don't need a code of ethics," he declared, "they have values."

Morita was making an important point, one in which an oft-noted cultural difference came into focus. American corporations are notoriously law-driven. Compliance to principle and policy is considered the core theme in corporate ethics. Japanese business, on the other hand, operates on the assumption that relationships and mutual understandings are first and foremost, and in such relationships rules and principles are at best secondary or even out of place. Their very existence suggests that something essential is missing, namely personal virtues and a real understanding of what is important. At worst, one might even see codes of ethics as a desperate corrective for an organization that has already gone dangerously astray.

Or, to put the point in a more positive way, one might think of a corporate code of ethics as ultimately nothing more than a description of the actual values and virtues manifested in the behavior of the corporation and its members. It is more like a mirror or a portrait than a rule book. In this sense, it is wholly dispensable.

Instead of thinking of corporate codes as top–down impositions from upper management or the powers that be, suppose that we think about codes as collective work in progress, an aspect of team building and self-affirmation. I have worked with several major corporations in developing a code of ethics, a set of values, a mission statement, and I have observed many more. It typically takes several months, even the better part of a year, and, in fact, it should take this long. There is the predictable amount of squabbling and grandstanding, redotting of i's and different imaginative crossings of t's, but the remarkable thing is: *they all come out the same.* Inevitably, what emerges is a prominent dedication to the customers; a cooperative conception of the community; an affirmation of respect for the individual; the now de rigieur emphasis on "teamwork"; some reference to innovation, initiative, or entrepreneurship; and an insistence on integrity (of course).

The hottest debate is almost always whether "return to the stockholders" should be part of the code, or whether this can simply be taken for granted. If it is included, the debate is how: Should it read "reasonable return" or "maximum return" or "fair return"? Usually, it is just left out as assumed. Some companies insist on being "the Best," but most more humbly "strive for excellence." Corporate codes are not the place to look for originality, but I have learned to keep this to myself. It is the process that counts. Nothing does a corporate community more good than the active, collective thinking about their own values and purpose. It is not surprising that the results, the virtues upon which good companies pride themselves, are pretty much the same.

Do corporate codes of ethics work? The answer to that often-asked question depends what is meant by it, and what kind of a company as well as what kind of a code we are talking about. If one believes the purpose of a corporate code is to hammer employees and managers into shape and convert cynical, disloyal, borderline criminals into God-fearing, moral men and women, then the answer, of course, is that no code—not even a fully sanctioned criminal code—can do that. If, on the other hand, one accepts the company code as an expression of the actual day-to-day working values of the employees and managers of the company, then it is not entirely clear what it means for the company code to "work," although it does accurately portray the company in its best light and reminds everyone what they are there to do.

Of the most critical importance, however, is the example set by the executives at the top. If they are seen to ignore the principles and provisions of the code in their own behavior, there is not a chance that anyone else who works for the company is going to take the code seriously. One can and should, of course, back up the specifics of the code with punishments—demotions and firings at the extreme. But having a code "with teeth," although essential if the code is to be taken seriously, does not mean that the success of the code should be measured by the number of violations that are punished (the prosecutor's accounting measure). In those hard cases where the code of ethics is created in order to make radical changes in the behavior of a company and its employees, it is not just the content of the code that must be carefully crafted. It is rather the culture of the entire company.

Business as a Profession

> The business person must see herself as a professional and the
> service motive must dominate. Business can only really do well if
> it seeks to do good.
> —Norman Bowie[50]

People in business should think of themselves as professionals. To already-professional managers, this may seem obvious, though a few business critics may find it outrageous.[51] The aim, once again, is to humanize our thinking and get away from narrow and destructive images of grubby individual competitiveness. Business, in the better way to think about it, is essentially a social enterprise, in which respectability and social responsibility are essential. Of course, people in business are there to make money, but making money and the need to make money are also common to the practices of medicine and engineering, and no one but a hopeless cynic would say that the essence of these professions is the quest for financial gain. Business, I want to argue, should also be considered a profession. Making money is the reward but not the goal of dedication and a job well done.

Discussions of business as a profession often refer back to a list of seven criteria borrowed from Abraham Flexner:[52]

1　Possess and draw upon a store of knowledge that is more than ordinarily complex.
2　Secure a theoretical grasp of the phenomenon with which it deals.
3　Apply its theoretical and complex knowledge to the practical solution of human and social problems.
4　Strive to add to and improve its stock of knowledge.
5　Pass on what it knows to novice generations; not in a haphazard fashion but deliberately and formally.
6　Establish criteria of admission, legitimate practice, and proper conduct.
7　Be imbued with an altruistic spirit.

Many of these characteristics concern the specialized knowledge and skills that a professional must have. A doctor, to say the obvious, needs extensive study in the anatomy and physiology of the body and the many malaises it suffers. But it seems to me that the complexities of modern accounting and financial analysis, to name but two of many such business specialties, are such that there can be no valid claim that business lacks similarly special knowledge and skills essential to a profession. When one adds (as one should) the considerable knowledge of operations, organization, and management that is becoming necessary to feel at home in almost any industry, it should be obvious that business is and should be regarded as a profession.

With the accumulation of knowledge and skill in any profession, there is also the need to pass this knowledge and these skills on. Education again becomes a critical ingredient in the specification of a profession, and a professional is, as such, concerned not just with his or her own competence but with the competence of succeeding generations and his or her own colleagues. Professions, accordingly, impose requirements and credentials on their practitioners, which determine who may and may not practice. One might object that this interferes with the free market, but the obvious counterargument is that self-regulation is not a fetter, and no profession or enterprise can long survive without it. A profession, as any public enterprise, has a reputation to defend. In medicine, quacks and frauds destroy trust and make trouble for everyone. Why shouldn't business be similarly protective of its reputation, and why should not people in business be similarly concerned with the impact of not only their own products on customers and on the society but those of the other companies as well? Ultimately, we're all in the same boat, and the leaks drown not only the guilty but all of us.

Thinking about business as a profession is particularly well illustrated in the heartfelt list produced by several participants at one of my recent seminars at Chase Manhattan Bank, discussing their own corporate values. Here is how they collectively defined the value called "professionalism":

1 Stay current and knowledgeable.
2 Accept and understand your responsibilities.
3 Take reponsibility for consequences and follow through.
4 Be willing to deal with the less rewarding aspects of the job.
5 Scrutinize yourself and seek improvement.
6 Have integrity; be ethical.
7 Present a good appearance; make a good impression.

And they not only recognized this value in their organization; they lived it as a personal virtue as well.

The Harvard Business School has as its motto, "To Make Business a Profession." Norman Bowie suggests that people in business should see themselves as "professionals rather than mere profit maximizers."⁵³ This is the heart of my "Aristotelian" argument here. We have heard quite enough about the pursuit of profits and the all-important bottom line. It is time to turn our attention to what business actually accomplishes in the world and not just the rewards that it accumulates in return.

Business, Merit, and Excellence

> Unfortunately, you don't get what you deserve, you get what you negotiate.
>
> —Dr. Chester L. Karrass

Excellence has long been a buzzword in business, a marketing term rather than a definition of purpose. Like *quality* (its close kin), it implies good value without any particular substance or commitment. But, both practically and philosophically, it is a word of great significance and indicates a sense of mission, a commitment beyond profit potential and the bottom line. It is a word that suggests "doing well" but also "doing good." It is a word, therefore, that synthesizes the demands of the marketplace and the demands of ethics. It might be worth noting that the Greek word *areté* is sometimes translated as "virtue" and sometimes as "excellence," and that ambiguity is significant. So it is assumed, in Aristotle's accounts of the virtues, that success and happiness will be commensurate with excellence.

In business life, the idea is that excellence sells, that excellence is the key to success. In other words, our emphasis on excellence also presupposes a particular sense of justice, a *meritocracy*, in which merit—excellence—is rewarded in the marketplace. Obviously, this is not always so, but the linkage between excellence and success is so important that it deserves some protracted scrutiny.

The business world is a meritocracy in that one expects reward in return for contribution. There may be a sizable element of luck involved as well as skills and talents that give some people considerable advantage over others, but one is rewarded for his or her contribution, whether or not it involves great insight or skill. (The reward for risk in investing, for example, may be independent of any work or skill whatever.) Nevertheless, the correlation between hard work, skill, and success is so convincing that we cannot conceive of our free enterprise system without it. Though it may be true that some great fortunes have been made through dumb luck and mere bumbling, the heart of the free enterprise system remains not luck but pluck—knowledge, skill, and hard work.

One of the critical problems in corporate life, and in the free market system in general, is the apparent failure of meritocracy, along with the increasing suspicion that hard work is not rewarded and good ideas are more likely to be ignored or stolen than compensated. Position becomes more important than ability or skill. "Schmoozing" and "going along to get along" replace productivity as the way to success. Personal public relations and publicity become more prudential than the project that actually gets developed. Indeed, the fast-tracking ideal often involves the mere plan of a project, just enough to demonstrate one's abilities (and allow one to move along) and just far enough along to cause considerable disruption and confusion in one's abandoned position or company.

In the wake of massive downsizing and the uncertainty of many mergers, executives and employees alike are losing faith in their own abilities to get ahead on their merits. This is a disaster, for both the companies and the country. Strategies for survival start to replace devotion to tasks. Research and development are displaced by the search for short-term results. Managers worry less about their effectiveness and much more about their appearance and placement. Virtue may be its own reward, but if it is not also rewarded, it may well turn a resentful cheek. There is nothing more destructive to productivity than interoffice resentment, envy, and spite.

Of particular concern here is the peculiar nature of managerial talent and skills. The skills involved in good management are not always so evident as the tangible results of a trade or profession such as carpentry, computer programming, or accounting. Management skills are people skills, matters of facilitation, and, at their best, inspirational. Thus an excellent manager knows that excellence in management is often evident in what does not happen or what seemingly happens with little effort rather than in any dramatic or breathtaking performance as such. (Indeed, breathtaking performances are often a symptom of an organization wildly out of control.) The best managers, accordingly, may be recognizable by the absence of troublesome situations rather than by any dramatic skill in fire fighting.

Consequently, the best managers may seem to sit by the sideline while others present their accomplishments to the world. The insecurity that inevitably results from this should not be taken to mean that excellence has no place in managerial life, however, or that management circles are by their very nature doomed (as some seem to be) to an insistent mediocrity, a "don't rock the boat" mentality. Managerial genius may also be manifested in productive anarchy, however, and we all know that the complete absence of any appearance of troublesome situations may be a sign of totalitarian mismanagement rather than anticipatory insight. It is necessary for top management to evaluate managerial performance without confusing flash for substance or silence for effectiveness.

Robert Jackall asks:

> What if men and women in the corporation no longer see success as necessarily connected to hard work? What becomes of the social morality of the corporation—the everyday rules-in-use that people play by—when there is thought to be no fixed or, one might say, objective standard of excellence to explain how and why winners are separated from also-rans, how and why some people succeed and others fail? What rules do people fashion to interact with one another when they feel that, instead of ability, talent, and dedicated service to an organization, politics, adroit talk, luck, connections, and self-promotion are the real sorters of people into sheep and goats?[54]

This is a critical question for a great many corporations today, not because corporations or their executives do not care about merit, but because a manager works in a nexus of interlocking responsibilities and the contribution of any one person may be impossible to ascertain. (Indeed, that is the very meaning of the much-touted word *teamwork*.) Rewarding merit is the first and foremost criterion for fairness, a virtue without which even the most successful organizations will become snake pits of bitterness and resentment.

The Meaning of Leadership [55]

[George] Washington, almost from the moment of his death, became a legend symbolizing (among other things) the "superiority" of American military leaders over foreign officers because of their great strength of character.
—Ernest Greenwood[56]

In order to collect the people, a leader must first collect himself.
—I Ching (1500 BCE)

What is leadership? The most common view is that it is *power*. Power, of course, is not irrelevant. It follows leadership, almost by definition. It sometimes paves the way for leadership. But power is not leadership, and leadership is not power. Coercion and mind control are powerful forms of authority and control, but we rightly refuse to call them "leadership." Hitler was a leader, but only insofar as he won the approval of his people, not because of his fascist control mechanisms, his force of arms, or his autocracy. Gandhi was a leader, despite the fact that he lacked arms and political power.

There are corporate bosses who rule through fear. They are not leaders. There are business leaders who exert very little control. They do not have to. They lead by virtue of their virtues. But what are these virtues that make good and sometimes great leaders? A thorough study, obviously, is beyond the scope of this book. But a few good words are in order, if only to clear a space within which the true virtues of leadership can be appreciated.

Leadership is essentially an *emotional relationship*. Which emotions, of course, is the crucial question, and here Machiavelli's classical cynicism immediately comes back to haunt us. "Whether 'tis better to be loved or feared," he asks, and opts for fear. We, on the other hand, opt for love, or at least some set of similarly positive emotions, and we reject fear as a basis for leadership. As Harry Truman once wisely said, "A leader is one who has the ability to get other people to do what they don't want to do, and *like* it." That is certainly not true of fear.

The emotional nature of leadership is often reduced to a simple virtue called charisma. The word *charisma* is often used as shorthand for the emotional power of exceptional leaders, but it is, unfortunately, a concept without ethical value and without much explanatory value either. Yet, it is one of the most frequently recurrent terms in current discussions of leadership. It comes (in its current usage) from the German sociologist Max Weber. It is, to its credit, just about the only term that so explicitly refers to the emotional nature of leadership, but, unfortunately, at considerable cost to clarity, imbued as the term is with a sense of mystery and magic. It connotes an irrational as opposed to a rational influence, although Weber himself was famous for his analysis of rationality. Nevertheless, he also saw rationality in terms of a costly disenchantment with the world, and at the end of his most famous book, *The Protestant Ethic and the Spirit of Capitalism*, he argued that rationalism is an "iron cage" in which both freedom and meaning are sacrificed to efficiency. One should not be surprised, therefore, that charisma came to offer a significantly religious promise for him.[57]

The theological dimension of the term (as its etymology, as "blessed," "graced by God") means that charisma is by its very nature a rare, very special quality. It does not invite analysis, and even such careful analytic writers as Robert Nozick are reduced to such impoverished New Age metaphors as an aura.[58] The fact that it is rare (and blessed) seems to invite gratitude and reverence rather than critical analyisis, and its kinship to magnetism and charm tends to foreclose any meaningful investigation. Indeed, James MacGregor Burns warns that the "term is so overused it threatens to collapse under close analysis."[59]

Bernard Bass describes charisma as displayed by leaders "to whom followers form deep emotional attachments and who in turn inspire their followers to transcend their own interests for superordinate goals."[60] True, perhaps, but what are these emotional attachments? The mysterious origins of charisma invite a serious worry: What if the gift is from Satan, not God?[61] Charisma can be a dangerous genie to let out of the bottle.

Weber celebrated charisma precisely for its spontaneity and freedom, its sense of "sovereignty" that was so at odds with institutions and rational methods. He opposed "charismatic" authority to "rational–legal" and "traditional" authority, where the former is the paradigm of institutions, the latter rather the paradigm of communities and more "natural" organizations.[62] Compared to rational–legal authority, charismatic leadership was irrational, and there can be little doubt that such was the quality that drew Weber—as so many of his German predecessors and successors—to it. But the term quickly became unanalyzable, overly poetic and romantic. In fact, it is a term that designates nothing in particular, except, perhaps, "a rare personal quality" of leaders "who arouse fervent popular devotion and enthusiasm."[63] But that is precisely what we want to understand.

The emphasis on charisma, however, should be replaced by the much more mundane notion of *trust*. Whereas charisma is celebrated as a mysterious attribute of a leader, trust, obviously, is a relationship between a leader and his or her followers. The practical applications will, I hope, be obvious. The focus on leadership will bear fruit only if, unlike some lovelorn cowboys, we don't go looking for leaders in all the wrong places.[64]

I began by stating that leadership should not be confused with power. I want to suggest that leadership begins rather with integrity and the virtues, in particular, those virtues that allow a leader to articulate the emotions and aspirations of others, to inspire them with trust and hope. Needless to say, this will result in "influence." It will also (almost inevitably) result in a kind of power, but it would be cynical to say "power over others." It is more like power with them, or through them, or for them. *Empowerment*, the most abused buzzword of the 1990s, is really what leadership is all about. But it does not mean *giving power over* (much less delegating responsibility without the authority to carry it through) nor even *sharing power* so much as it is the mutual *creation of power*, power through hope, power through trust, through the power of a shared vision.

Leadership, in other words, is the very opposite of control, and to say that leadership is a matter of emotions is not to say that it is a matter of emotional control or, for that matter, emotional manipulation either. Control is a quasi-mechanical term, and, in human relationships, it implies at the very least some sort of coercion, which virtually every leadership theorist has rightly distinguished from leadership. Leadership through naked terror, imperatives backed up by threats, is not leadership. Military commanders who threaten to shoot their own troops if they retreat are not leaders, nor are executives who threaten to fire or demote their employees. So, too, manipulating emotions, as if they were circuits to simply be stimulated, is not leadership either. Zombies and robots may be commanded to behave without reference to their will, but we do not think of someone as a loyal follower if he or she is merely a zombie or a robot.

When we say that the true leader articulates the visions, hopes, and other passions of the people led, we need not mean that he or she completely understands exactly what he or she is doing. Just as people need not know the direction in which they are being led, it does not follow that the leaders themselves know the direction in which they are leading. Hegel captured that lack of clarity in his stunning phrase, "the cunning of reason," and Leo Tolstoy illustrated it in his unflattering treatment of even the principals in the 1812 Napoleonic invasion of Russia. The leader may well be "feeling his way along" or "following his intuitions," and his followers may know only that they trust him and that they are faithfully following. But what defines leadership is the articulation of the appropriate emotions and the inspiration of trust, and this will often be an overriding passion to do the right thing.

Being and Doing: The Nature of the Virtues

> It staggers me that for whatever reason being nice is seen as being inconsistent with being tough.
> —Craig Weatherup, CEO, Pepsico[65]

We are an action-and-results society, which is why we so readily accede to moral theories and corporate reviews that evaluate our actions and their consequences. But behind every action, and prior to the consequences of action, is the *person*, the personality, who is not just an agent but a *human being*. Before we can *do*, we must *be*, even if what we become, not surprisingly, is the accumulation and outcome of, among other things, our actions. But that means that among the consequences of our actions, indeed, foremost among them or prior to them, we must keep in mind who we are and what we are making of ourselves, our own ideals, and how we see ourselves and how others see us, too.

A virtue, in essence, is a value embodied and built into action. A virtue, accordingly, is an excellent characteristic to have, not just in some narrowly defined context (as it is a virtue to be ugly in an "ugliest man contest") but in the larger social scheme of things. The concept of the virtues provides the conceptual linkage between the individual and his or her society. A virtue is a pervasive trait of character that allows one to fit into a particular society, even to excel in it. Aristotle analyzed the virtues as the basic constituents of happiness, and these virtues included, we should add right away, not only such moral virtues as honesty but also many nonmoral virtues such as wittiness, generosity, and loyalty. (Aristotle, in fact, did not even bother distinguishing between the moral and the nonmoral virtues. He considered them all important.) The virtues were, on the one hand, essential aspects of the individual. On the other hand, they were precisely the "excellences" that a certain society required. The underlying assumption was that a person is who he or she is by virtue of his or her place and role in the community, by virtue of his or her actions and sense of judgment, by virtue of how his or her virtues all work together to form what we might blandly call "a good person."

In modern society, being a good person means—in any of a large number of senses—being a productive person, making a contribution. Adam Smith's best friend, the great Scottish philosopher David Hume, said that a virtue is a trait that is both pleasing and useful to ourselves and pleasing and useful to others. Honesty is obviously such a virtue. If everyone lied—to begin with one of the oldest and most obvious philosophical insights—no one would believe anyone. There will always be liars, and there are practices that encourage and even require less than forthright disclosure, but there could not be a society of liars, even where the telling of lies is notoriously widespread (e.g., in Hollywood, where everyone understands why Lynda Rosen Obst would entitle her recent book, *Hello, He Lied*[66], or in current-day American politics).

Courage is a virtue. There will always be cowards, but most of us at some time or other have to stand up for our convictions and our freedom. Otherwise, we have no convictions and there is no freedom. But in addition to these rather general virtues, there are also virtues specific to particular institutions, activities, and practices. Spontaneous creativity and unpredictable behavior may be applauded in an artist or an intellectual, but it is (usually) disastrous in a linebacker. Loyalty is almost always a virtue within a relationship or an organization, but it is a virtue that has its obvious limits ("My company, right or wrong, displays the importance of such limits, even in their denial"). Virtues may be specific to particular institutions, activities, and practices, but virtue will always be measured in a larger arena.

Sometimes, that arena needs to be enlarged considerably, to include all of humanity or, even, all of nature. The virtues of being a good Nazi, we must insist, are not virtues at all. They may mock the virtues, obedience and patriotism, for instance, but, in the larger human context, they are the vices of blind obedience and chauvinism, jingoism, xenophobia, imperialism. So, too, being productive in one's job is a virtue only if the larger consequences are benign. More problematic and controversial, we might say that some of the virtues of being a good citizen in an ecologically irresponsible society are so only insofar as they lend themselves to the flourishing of not only the society but of the natural environment as well. How far we want to take this, of course, is going to be a matter of continuing debate and concern, but the virtue of the virtues, we might say, is never just local. They harmonize people with each other and with the whole of society, the whole of humanity, or even the whole of the cosmos.

Nevertheless, the virtues tend to be context-bound, relative to various practices and activities, and that means that new practices will produce new virtues, as the new practice of business investment encouraged by John Calvin produced a new and novel virtue called "thrift." The particular virtues of business have to do with the particular purpose of the business establishment, not just to make money but to serve society's demands and the public good (and be properly rewarded for doing so). Thus the mission of the corporation might best be conceived as its own statement of the virtues and the purposes that define those virtues. "Better living through chemistry," "Quality at a good price," "Productivity through people," "Progress is our most important product"—these are not mere advertising slogans but reasons for working and for living.

Without such a mission, a company is without a purpose and is a liability to the society around it. Just being in business may, unintentionally, contribute to the public good, but Adam Smith's "invisible hand" never was a very reliable social strategy.[67] The difference between intending to do good and doing good unintentionally is not just the special sense of satisfaction that comes from the former. Contrary to the utterly irresponsible and obviously implausible argument that those ("do-gooders") who try to do good in fact do more harm than good, the simple, self-evident truth is that most of the good in this world (and not the road to Hell) comes about through good intentions. Meaningful human activity is that which intends the good rather than stumbling over it on the way to merely competitive or selfish goals.

In business, what is called "ruthlessness" can be a virtue, but only insofar as it ultimately serves moral and utilitarian purposes. Thus ruthlessness in the defense of other virtues might itself be a virtue, but ruthlessness just for the sake of intimidation and control is a vice. The virtue of a virtue (a phrase I borrow from Nietzsche) always depends on the larger context, a context in which the practice itself (art, football, business) is evaluated for its social and moral value. In the business world, in particular, we should be on the lookout for those mock-virtues that in the larger society would and should be subject to ridicule and contempt. Thus when Michael Lewis describes the ideal of the traders at Salomon Brothers as "that most revered of all species: a Big Swinging Dick," we realize that we have lowered ourselves to an adolescent conception of business virtue that is by no means worth defending.[68]

Not all virtues need be serious. Aristotle listed charm, wit, and a good sense of humor as virtues, and I think that we would probably agree. To be sure, the circumstances in which congeniality is a central virtue and in which courage becomes cardinal will be very different, but it is a troubled organization that requires the more heroic virtues all the time and does not have the relative security and leisure to enjoy those virtues that make life worthwhile rather than those that are necessary for mere survival. Indeed, part of the folly of the familiar military, machine, and jungle metaphors in business is that they all make business life out to be something threatening and relentless. But the truth (even in the military and in the jungle) is that there are long and sometimes relaxed respites and a need for play and playfulness as well as diligence. There is welcome camaraderie, and the virtues of "getting along" are just as important to group survival as the coordination needed for fighting together. There are reasons why we want to survive—apart from sheer Darwinian obstinacy—and the fact that we relish and enjoy the social harmony of our lives and our jobs is one of them. One of the most powerful but most ignored arguments against hostile takeovers and unfriendly mergers is the desire on the part of the members of a corporate community to maintain that community, and this is undermined when executives feel they have to fight to keep their jobs.

Business ethics is too often conceived as a set of impositions and constraints, obstacles to business behavior rather than the motivating force of that behavior. So conceived, it is no surprise that many people in business look upon ethics and ethicists with suspicion, as antagonistic if not antithetical to their enterprise. But properly understood, ethics does not and should not consist of a set of prohibitive principles or rules. It is the virtue of an ethics of virtue to be rather an *intrinsic* part and the driving force of a successful life well lived.

Business ethics is not just or primarily the study of right and wrong, any more than art and aesthetics involve only beauty and ugliness.[69] Ethics (like art and aesthetics) is a colorful, multifaceted appreciation and engagement with other people in the world. In business ethics, it is only the extreme and sinister misdeed that we label simply "wrong"; even then, we are likely to invoke an artist's palette of imaginative descriptions such as "sleazy" and "slimy." Even the phrase "good character" (or "good person") strikes us as ultimately vacuous; it is the individual details that count. And there are many, many details—many, many virtues. It is to some of them that we now turn.

PART III
A Catalog of Business Virtues

In Chinese philosophy, the word for "virtue" (Chinese: *Te*) is sometimes translated as "potency." It is an apt image because a virtue is a kind of power. It is one's potential. It is that which enables us to become who we really are. But who we are depends upon the roles we play in life, and the virtues that count the most are those that help us along our way (Chinese: *Tao*).

In business, "the way" involves such activities as exchanging goods and services, making money, and dealing with other people's needs and demands. Consequently, business has built into it such notions as mutual agreement and the expectation of honest dealing and fair exchange. Thus we might identify the three most basic business virtues: *honesty, fairness,* and *trustworthiness.* These are the virtues that empower, that make business possible. There can be no business arrangement, no business society, that does not presuppose these. Peter Drucker, in his classic tome *Management*, says that the one essential feature of a good manager is integrity. But integrity, as we have seen, is not a single feature nor a single virtue but an encapsulation, the unity of virtues. And of those virtues, we would do well to highlight honesty, fairness, and trustworthiness.

In the catalog of the virtues that follows, however, we will not try to order the virtues in any kind of list of priority. Rather, the strategy will be to let the virtues fall where they may, which happens here to be English alphabetical order, and to understand their similarities and differences. There is no need to insist that some virtues are more important than others, and the catalog can be utilized in any number of individualized ways. The reader is encouraged to browse at his or her own pace, rather than pursuing the virtues "from Ability to Zeal."

For each virtue, I have specified the context in which it is pertinent (integrity, as the summary virtue, being pertinent in all). Courage, for example, is appropriate to those situations in which there is danger, whether the danger is being killed, being fired, being reprimanded, not being promoted, or just being embarrassed or humiliated.

Then I suggest the basic concern or concerns of that virtue. In the case of "toughness," for instance, the basic concern is not being beaten down or defeated by opposing forces, temptations, or arguments. In trustworthiness, the basic concern is to be worthy of trust, to be the sort of person who can be trusted.

Every virtue has a rich mythology, whether by way of cautionary tales (the myth of King Midas) or idealizations (Socrates, Jesus). But myths need not be taken from ancient folktales or religion. We live our real-life myths all of the time, with paradigm scenarios or exemplary cases that form the prototypes of the behavior we expect of ourselves and others. Without pretending to even scratch the surface here, I have tried to make a suggestion or two about how we envision these virtues.

The Scottish philosopher David Hume defined the virtues in terms of their usefulness, both to oneself and to others. I have argued throughout that the virtue of the virtues is that they do not polarize self-interest and others' interests, so this seems to be a good place to point out how self-interest and the interest of others converge in the virtues. I suggest ways in which each virtue is useful both to oneself and to others.

Aristotle suggested that a virtue is "the mean between the extremes," which he demonstrated by noting the excess and deficiency of each virtue, that is, what goes wrong when the basic concern goes off target. Sometimes, this excess or deficiency is tantamount to vice (e.g., cowardice or stinginess), but by no means always. I thus note an excess and deficiency for each virtue.

Finally, I suggest an "acid test," not in the strict chemical sense of that term, of course, nor as the definitive focus for each and every virtue. Rather, I have in mind a somewhat tongue-in-cheek "for instance," sometimes opposing the true exercise of a virtue as opposed to its merely superficial performance (e.g., friendliness that turns nasty under pressure, or courage that betrays itself as mere bravado in the face of danger).

Needless to say, the list is not complete. Indeed, there are literally hundreds of virtues (or virtues named) in English, not to mention those recognized by other cultures without English equivalents or translations. I have generally represented whole families of virtues (e.g., honesty, openness, candor, frankness, sincerity, truthfulness) with a single virtue (e.g., honesty). I do not mean to imply that these are identical by any means, only that they are related. (The difference between honesty and sincerity, for example, could take up a chapter all alone.) This brief catalog is meant to present a general overview of the virtues and their place in business life.

Ability

Context: things to be done, in other words, virtually any concrete human situation
Basic Concern(s): getting the thing done and done well
Myth: Mr(s). Fix-it, a black belt in competence
Useful to Self: effectiveness in living, pride, confidence
Useful to Others: dependability, competence, effectiveness, admiration (onvy?)
Excess: overconfidence, arrogance
Deficiency: incompetence
Acid Test: "But I've never done that before."

Perhaps we should start with a nonmoral virtue to make an important point, that thinking of business and ethics in terms of the virtues cuts across the ultimately false divide between skills and morals. Ethics, like business, is a practice (or a large set of practices) in which competence as well as good intentions are essential. Ability refers not just to talent, of course, but to the cultivated products of training, education, and conscientiousness. To do good, one needs to be able to do well.

Acceptance

Context: difficult or frustrating situations (in other words, life)
Basic Concern(s): making the best of a bad situation
Myth: Sisyphus pushing his rock up the mountain for the 12,875,425th time (Albert Camus, in the *Myth of Sisyphus*: "He makes the rock 'his thing' ")

Useful to Self: attunement to the world, satisfaction with self, contentment
Useful to Others: not making impossible demands, cutting down on whining and complaints
Excess: "quitter," giving up too easily, not changing something that really ought to be changed, lack of imagination
Deficiency: hitting one's head against a brick wall, continuous frustration
Acid Test: Accepting the fact that you are always going to have to live with . . .

Acceptance isn't a virtue pure and simple, of course. Resigning oneself to things as they are, when things are clearly not as they should be, may be a desperate strategy, after all attempts to change things have failed and there is no promising possibility anywhere on the horizon. All too often, acceptance as resignation signals a weakness of imagination or an unwillingness to persevere in the face of difficulty. But there are times, especially when the stakes are low, that giving up is no vice but rather a sure sign of wisdom. Accepting one's talents and one's lot in life, including its misfortunes and failures, is one of the pillars of wisdom most recommended by many of the great religious thinkers and philosophers in history.

Ambition

Context: career advancement
Basic Concern(s): getting ahead
Myth: Horatio Alger stories, in which the stockboy works his way up to being CEO, the immigrant entrepreneur who, with three dollars in his pocket, builds a financial empire
Useful to Self: motivationally effective, clarity of direction if not always goals
Useful to Others: predictability, tenacity, know what offers and requests to make
Excess: ambition is sometimes its own excess, when it loses sight of the larger context and humility (Cassius, in Shakespeare's *Julius Caesar*: "Such men are dangerous")

Deficiency: apathy, indifference, lack of motivation
Acid Test: How much will you put up with for a promotion?
How much hardship and effort for another step up the
ladder?

It is worth including this dubious or at any rate two-faced virtue. In the United States, ambitiousness is highly lauded and associated with motivation and persistence. In many cultures, however, ambitiousness is seen as a vice, as not just motivation but ruthlessness, a dangerous form of greed. What is considered more virtuous is a certain acceptance of one's lot in life (cf. **Acceptance**). Insofar as ambitiousness implies vision, motivation, and stick-to-itiveness, we can agree that it is a virtue, but insofar as it suggests callousness and lack of interest in or attention to the well-being of others and ruthlessness, it turns out to be its own vice.

Amiability (Friendliness)

Context: virtually all interpersonal contacts
Basic Concern(s): to put others at ease
Myth: Mr. Nice Guy, Ms. Congeniality, the one who (almost)
never frowns
Useful to Self: fosters agreeable social contexts
Useful to Others: fosters agreeable social contexts
Excess: unctuousness, intrusiveness
Deficiency: coldness, aloofness, indifference
Acid Test: Smile maintained even after scuffing the blue
suede shoes.

Business is first of all interpersonal activity concerned with mutual satisfaction of needs and desires. Accordingly, its virtues are those that are essential to interpersonal relationships, to the recognition of mutual needs and desires, and to the satisfaction of those needs and desires. Amiability, congeniality, and friendliness are therefore high on the list of business virtues. Like many virtues, the importance of friendliness is most obvious in the breach, and if friendliness sometimes seems like a vice in business, it is only because it is so routine that it often works as a cover for more devious motives and, on occasion, for viciousness. The very particular business virtue of "salesmanship" contains a huge measure of friendliness, not only as a successful technique but as essential to the activity itself. More generally, the atmosphere of friendliness that pervades any congenial company is essential to the kind of cooperation that any organization requires.

Friendliness is one of Aristotle's most celebrated virtues, but we should be cautious about equating Aristotle's virtue with the trait that is prized in the corporate business community. Aristotle's virtue is not at all our slap-a-stranger-on-the-back-and-give-a-big-smile sense of friendliness. Friendliness for Aristotle refers more to *being* a friend than to any superficial feeling or expression of friendship. Aristotle does not mean being friendly to everybody. For Aristotle, friendliness is selective, even snobbish, not general congeniality that every employee of a company is expected to display from nine to five. But we, too, might distinguish genuine friendship from friendliness. Friendship is one of our most important personal values, and it is very different from and extraneous to the friendliness expected in the corporation.

Nevertheless, working as hard as we do and for so many hours, it is not surprising that many people form their closest friendships with colleagues at the office. But such friendships are not part of one's corporate responsibilities—even in a designated mentor or "buddy" relationship. Indeed, an extremely close friendship on the job may even be a disruption or an invitation to injustice (cronyism).

Articulateness

Context: presentations, negotiations, arguments, explanations

Basic Concern(s): to make one's case, to allow others to understand, to express oneself

Myth: Socrates, who could talk anyone into agreement (or, at least, submission); Shakespeare's Marc Antony, who in a single speech consolidated the opinion of all Rome to his cause

Useful to Self: get clear about one's own ideas and feelings, win over others

Useful to Others: being understood, clearly; helping to clarify their ideas and feelings, too; coordinating and expressing a sense of solidarity (teamwork)

Excess: garrulousness, pretentiousness

Deficiency: vagueness, unstructured emotional response, confusing and alienating others (cf. Billy Budd, Melville's sailor, committed murder because he could not express himself clearly)

Acid Test: "Explain why you allowed a drunken sea captain to be in charge of that oil tanker." (The CEO failed the test.)

Business is a distinctively human activity because it is a distinctively *linguistic* activity. Whatever else it may be—the production of products, the honing of skills, and the working of numbers—business is talk, conversation, negotiation, making offers and requests, and making and keeping promises and commitments. Articulateness is nothing less than being able to express oneself, and consequently one's offers, requests, promises, and commitments, clearly and forcefully. One might say that it is a skill rather than a virtue, and that it can, of course, be put to bad use. But it is so essential to the practice of business, so essential to honesty and forthrightness, to explaining and justifying the ethical twists of business decisions, to understanding as well as expressing oneself and one's feeling, that it deserves inclusion here (cf. **Ability**).

Attentiveness

Context: any project, meeting, gathering

Basic Concern(s): to listen, to understand, to get it right

Myth: Joseph listening to Pharaoh, Sigmund Freud hearing much more than is said

Useful to Self: to know what's going on

Useful to Others: to be respected, to be heard, to have one's concerns taken seriously

Excess: intrusiveness, compulsiveness

Deficiency: sloppiness, carelessness, indifference, rudeness

Acid Test: Your customer is too polite to say what she really needs.

Perhaps the most underrated virtue in business is *listening well*. It is basic to trust and being trusted, essential to knowing what's going on—an important virtue as well as an essential skill. Attention to details is often the difference between success and disaster. In a sense, all business is attentiveness, listening to your customers—and potential customers.

Autonomy

Context: all moral, decision-making social contexts (e.g., in a corporation)

Basic Concern(s): personal responsibility, personal identity, personal integrity

Myth: in *Twelve Angry Men*, the lone juror who won't go along with the crowd

Useful to Self: essential to one's sense of self, not being dragged along unthinkingly

Useful to Others: knowing where you stand

Excess: rebelliousness, self-righteousness

Deficiency: going along with the crowd, lack of self, inauthenticity

Acid Test: "Everyone else has voted in favor of this [disastrous] measure. How about you?"

Autonomy is independence, independence of thinking, independence of action. To be in an organization is, to be sure, to "follow the party line." But the question of autonomy is the question, "Whom do you really follow?" and the answer is "Yourself and your values." Autonomy does not mean making decisions in a vacuum or in a context-free zone. We are all creatures of our upbringing, our parents, and our cultures, but within our contexts, autonomy requires carving out a space of our own, a space defined by our values that we will not allow to be violated.

Caring

Context: anywhere with other people on a regular basis, in any position of control and responsibility

Basic Concern(s): others' well-being
Myth: the boss who kept all of his employees on payroll when the factory burned down (and had the world's most loyal employees when it was rebuilt)
Useful to Self: empathy-satisfaction, winning trust and loyalty
Useful to Others: being cared for, security
Excess: paternalism, intrusiveness, mawkishness
Deficiency: indifference, callousness
Acid Test: The clerk in your office with a diagnosis of AIDS; your employees in a downturn.

Caring is not a term that gets executive hearts beating faster the way that *competition* and the *profit motive* do. Instead, it conjures up very uncorporate images of the nursery, the hospital, and, for those obsessed with costs, it immediately suggests enormous increases in health and retirement benefits. But much of the uninspiring imagery of caring has to do with the overly military and otherwise macho metaphors that have dominated so much of business thinking in this century and the relegation of "caring roles" to women who stayed at home. Caring, of course, is not incompatible with corporate thinking. The virtuous corporate leader necessarily cares for his or her people, just as a successful military commander cares for his troops. Indeed, when one thinks of the "survival of the fittest" imagery applied to the corporation, it becomes obvious that the fittest corporation will be one that cares for and nurtures its employees and managers.

Caring in the corporation consists of a fundamental attitude. That attitude is one of mutual affection and a corresponding sense of obligation. This does not mean mawkish sentiment, and it certainly does not suggest that the best executive is one who treats or thinks of his or her employees as children. It does mean that the recognition and treatment of one's employees as full-blooded people, full of fears and jealousies and other unbusinesslike emotions, is essential to the bonding that corporate life requires. It involves the recognition that a resentful employee is a minimally cooperative and potentially destructive employee, and that a fearful employee—especially if the fear is for his or her job—is an employee who cannot, despite appearances and efforts to the contrary, be expected to be loyal or dedicated. Caring is not just charity or selfless generosity. Caring is essential to the unity and the health of any ongoing organization. It is an investment in the future.

Care, broadly conceived, encompasses almost all emotions, insofar as one must care about the world in order to feel anything else about it. We can restrict our characterization of care, however, to include just those positive feelings about others such that one wants them to do well and is moved to act on their behalf. Caring without being moved to action is not caring but mere emotional voyeurism. To care for someone is itself a course of action, not merely a feeling. It ultimately means to help others grow and actualize themselves.[70]

Charisma

Context: leadership
Basic Concern(s): to inspire others
Myth: the Great Leader (e.g., either Roosevelt) who rouses the nation in a crisis
Useful to Self: wins others over
Useful to Others: focus, inspiration, invigoration
Excess: fascism, cultism
Deficiency: ineffectiveness
Acid Test: Getting people to go willingly, even enthusiastically, where they refused to go before.

Charisma has been identified, for example, by Max Weber, as the emotional essence of leadership, inspiring others to follow through difficult times and tasks. Unfortunately, charisma connotes an irrational as opposed to a rational influence, and the theological etymology of the term as "blessed" marks it by its very nature to be a rare, very special quality. Bernard Bass describes charisma as displayed by leaders "to whom followers form deep emotional attachments and who in turn inspire their followers to transcend their own interests for superordinate goals."

Compassion

Context: other people who are in trouble

Basic Concern(s): relieving their suffering
Myth: the good samaritan, the Buddha, Mother Teresa, Jesus
Useful to Self: others will reciprocate, sense of solidarity
Useful to Others: sympathetic, helpful
Excess: sentimentality, mawkishness, ineffectiveness, emotional paralysis, incompetent "do-goodism"
Deficiency: callousness, cruelty, indifference to the plight of others
Acid Test: The employee who has just lost a child; the employee who has just been let go.

The great Chinese philosopher Mencius wrote over two thousand years ago, "No man is devoid of a heart sensitive to the sufferings of others. . . . Whoever is devoid of the heart of compassion is not human."[71] Compassion literally means "feeling with," and thus it is often confused with "empathy" or "putting yourself in the other person's shoes." But one need not exercise such elaborate moral imagination in order to have compassion for others. Typically, compassion simply requires paying attention to the plight of other people. Compassion is the felt need to do something about it, or, at least, to stick by others in their time of need.

Compassion requires understanding, but, again, it would be a mistake to think that this need involve any great psychological insight or that it necessarily requires excessive tolerance. It doesn't take much of a psychological genius to recognize that another person is in pain or difficulty, and one need not approve (or refrain from disapproving) of the behavior that brought about the pain or difficulty. Within the corporation, compassion is often called for—once one looks up out of the ledger books or over the computer screen—for an employee who has a sick spouse or child, for a manager who has him- or herself just received an ominous medical report, for a colleague who manifests the signs of serious depression or a drinking problem.

Compassion, of course, can be expensive. Giving time off, paying for medical or counseling expenses, taking time off from work to express one's concern, but what is less obvious is the enormous expense of not having or expressing compassion, in further lost time and the distraction that comes of suffering through hardship alone, in the insecurity and consequent lack of devotion of not only the employee in question but of everyone around, in seething resentment. Compassion, like caring, is not merely a humanizing embellishment in the otherwise businesslike life of the corporation. It is essential to the very life of that corporation as a human community.

Competitiveness

Context: any social context with limited rewards, rule-governed rivalries, defined opposition
Basic Concern(s): to win, to do *comparatively* well
Myth: the Olympiad, American football as an allegory for everything
Useful to Self: motivating, inspiring, invigorating
Useful to Others: motivating, inspiring, invigorating
Excess: ruthlessness, poor sportsmanship, tendency to cheat or bypass the rules
Deficiency: ineffectiveness, being "run over," "loser"
Acid Test: "When the going gets rough . . . "

Competition, we have already learned, is not the primary dynamic of business, but it is indisputably essential to the workings of a free market. Competition makes the market "work." But competition in the marketplace always presumes a generally accepted network of rules and mores of "proper play," and there is both healthy and unhealthy competition. Competitiveness as a virtue is restrained by these rules and sensibilities and motivated, in part, by the sense that the larger cooperative context must be preserved. Darwinian competitiveness, on the other hand, defined by the fight for survival, is a poor and out-of-place metaphor for the necessarily civilized practice of business. Contrary to what the Great Coach said, winning is neither everything nor the only thing.

Contentment

Context: situations of seemingly unlimited temptation and opportunities
Basic Concern(s): happiness, peace of mind
Myth: "The wise man is satisfied with what he has." (Talmud)

Useful to Self: a healthy absence of excess ambition and frustration

Useful to Others: a healthy lack of excess ambition and excessive competitiveness

Excess: complacency, unimaginativeness, laziness, slothfulness

Deficiency: continuing frustration, dissatisfaction, pointless ambition

Acid Test: "If you had your life to live over, would you be satisfied with the same life?"

Contentment might not seem to be a virtue, especially in a world where ambitiousness is thought to be one, but there is real wisdom in knowing when enough is enough, not being greedy, and allowing oneself to simply be satisfied. To be sure, a world full of contented people does not seem very exciting (Nietzsche lambasted that world in his parable of "The Last Man" [in *Thus Spoke Zarathustra*], and Francis Fukuyama picked up on the image in his recent book, *The End of History and the Last Man*, in which the last man becomes the late-twentieth-century bourgeois consumer). But a world filled with people filled with ambition is an explosive and probably fatal situation, and, in a world still overpopulated with poverty and want, there are worse things to idealize than a world in which everyone has enough. On the other hand, to be contented with oneself without concern for those who are without is no virtue either (see also Acceptance).

Cool-Headedness

Context: emotionally charged situations

Basic Concern(s): to retain control, reasonableness, articulateness

Myth: grace under fire, "Mr. Cool," James Bond in most of the *007* movies

Useful to Self: to retain control, to stay reasonable

Useful to Others: reasonableness, security, confidence

Excess: coldness, indifference, callousness

Deficiency: hot-tempered, loss of control

Acid Test: Your boss gives the promotion you deserved to his nephew.

Passion may be a virtue, but not all passions pass the test. Anger and fear, especially in their extreme forms of rage and panic, can be debilitating and career-ending. "Keeping cool" is an enormously valuable virtue, so long as it doesn't turn into passionless indifference. But it is a strategic virtue, not the same as the virtue of contentment. It is self-control rather than stoic *apatheia*.

Cooperativeness (Teamwork)

Context: shared projects and goals
Basic Concern(s): to get the thing done
Myth: "one for all and all for one"
Useful to Self: more and better results than one could produce alone
Useful to Others: more and better results than one could produce alone
Excess: loss of autonomy
Deficiency: competitiveness, creation of mutual obstacles
Acid Test: The job everyone thinks that they could do better alone.

One key corporate virtue is one's ability and willingness to be a "team player." Even without the sports-inclined metaphor, this suggests cooperation and other group-minded virtues. In corporations, cooperation is essential for effectiveness, but even people in business for themselves quickly find that business necessarily consists of alliances and working together—with suppliers, people in the community, and, of course, customers. An overemphasis on competitiveness can too easily undermine the spirit of cooperation. An unfair or ill-conceived reward system can destroy even the most dedicated team.

Courage

Context: situations of threats and danger (being fired, not being promoted)

Basic Concern(s): to do the right thing (despite the cost)
Myth: Achilles, the great Greek warrior who knew no fear; Socrates, who stood up for what he believed, even in the face of death
Useful to Self: maintains one's integrity, avoids shame and guilt
Useful to Others: as inspiration, as example, someone who will do what others won't (but want to)
Excess: recklessness, foolishness, self-righteousness
Deficiency: cowardice
Acid Test: Your boss is adamant, but just plain wrong. No one else will say anything, but the probable results will be disastrous.

Most relevant here, in business, is what is often called *moral courage*, that is, the courage to make the difficult decision to do the right thing even in the face of serious threats or dangers. In business, the dangers are rarely to one's life, as in, say, the military, but rather to one's career or one's financial well-being. Without moral courage, many of the other virtues are no more than good intentions.

Creativity (Imagination)

Context: in the mire of the known and routine as well as in new and unfamiliar situations
Basic Concern(s): something better, something different
Myth: "In the beginning, God created . . . "; Thomas Edison; the person who invented the wheel; Jobs and Wozniak in their garage; Mahatma Gandhi
Useful to Self: to exercise one's best faculties, to be free beyond the fullness of the present, to go where no one has gone before
Useful to Others: inspiration, innovation, creation of the new
Excess: excessive fantasy, lack of relevance or realism
Deficiency: stuck in the mire
Acid Test: "There's no way!" "No one has ever been able to do that."

Creativity, on the one hand, is what free enterprise and entrepreneurship are all about, bringing into existence clever conveniences or much-needed necessities that were not there before. On the other hand, some of the worst prose in psychology, education, and business has been written on the subject of creativity, what it is and how to get it, so I will not add to it here. One thing for sure, "the mother of invention [may be] necessity," but creativity in any organization requires *freedom*, room to imagine, a sense that someone up there is listening. Just as important as innovation in the organization is sponsorship—if just allowing room for mistakes—from the top. But of particular importance is *moral* imagination, not taking ethical problems or solutions at face value but rather seeing beyond them, perhaps into new moral territory not considered before.

Determination (Persistence, "Stick-to-itiveness")

Context: in the midst of a task, a project, a campaign
Basic Concern(s): to see it through, to not give up or be a "quitter"
Myth: "On the 195th try, . . . "
Useful to Self: pride of persistence, trust from others, more likely to get things done
Useful to Others: more likely to get things done, being someone to depend on
Excess: obstinacy, stubbornness, not knowing when to give up
Deficiency: unwilling to try, easy resignation, stopped by the smallest obstacle or setback
Acid Test: When everyone else has given up, or "Just when you think it never will work, . . . "

Business involves risk and uncertainty. There are always obstacles to any deal. There is always an excuse to quit. Determination is nothing other than the will to see things through, the vision to see the possibility of success, the optimism to see that possibility as real.

Entrepreneurship

Context: a gap in the market
Basic Concern(s): "to go where no one has ever gone before"—and make a sale
Myth: Bill Gates, who turned a technical toy into a great corporation
Useful to Self: independence, a fortune to be made
Useful to Others: new ideas, new products, needs met (that no one knew were needs)
Excess: overly "pushy," ambitious, independent to the point of being obnoxious, uncooperative, unrealistic about the size or elasticity of the market or the worthiness of the product
Deficiency: lack of creativity, lack of vision, lack of will, lack of people skills
Acid Test: The refrigerator salesman at the North Pole. In general, finding customers.

Entrepreneurship is the virtue of choice in current business mythology, embracing as it does both independence and the sweet smell of success. But not all entrepreneurs are successful (does one have to actually say this?) and not all business is entrepreneurship. But the very word itself, a variation on "taking charge," suggests a quintessential business virtue. The real danger is excess idealization (or idolatry) and the mistaking of mere success (success by luck, success by force or viciousness) or individual obstinacy for entrepreneurship.

Fairness

Context: all dealings with other people, especially those in which one has some leverage or power
Basic Concern(s): to give each his or her due, to treat people both equally and with regard to their differences, to reward merit and to not reward unethical behavior
Myth: Ms. Justice with her scales and blindfold; Plato's Ring of Gyges, which turns its wearer invisible (the just person would not take advantage of that)

Useful to Self: a more harmonious world
Useful to Others: a more harmonious world
Excess: insisting on equality when some people clearly
   deserve more than others; King Solomon, offering to cut
   the baby in half to give each mother an equal share
Deficiency: favoritism; arbitrary, ideological adherence to a
   "theory" of justice rather than looking at the situation
Acid Test: You've got the power, but there isn't enough
   bonus money to go around.

In a sense, the whole point of mutual agreement is fairness. It is often assumed by legal and political thinkers that an agreement between knowledgeable, intelligent, informed, consenting adults is thereby fair, even if (from outside eyes) the balance of exchange is by no means equal and one person is getting a much better deal than the other. Of course, such an agreement may be compromised by coercion or what Hobbes called "Force and Fraud," but so long as the agreement itself is not extorted or compelled, the deal is generally considered valid. (There are exceptions, such as the high price of life-prolonging medicine for the desperately ill.)

Fairness is one of the most basic business virtues, also to be found under the more philosophically formidable title of "justice." Fairness isn't so much an ideal in business as a basic expectation. It has to do with honesty, dependability, and trust, insofar as mutual agreement is, in business, the hallmark of fairness. It also has to do with the notion of equivalence or equity, the value of what is exchanged, whether it be goods, work, or wages. But it is not as if "fair price" and "fair wages" and "reasonable returns" are marked in heaven, which once again brings us back to the importance of mutual agreement, which, writ large, is what we call "market value." (This sense of market has been and still is resisted.) Aristotle and Aquinas really did write as if prices and the wages of labor were somehow written into the nature of things, and even Adam Smith (and after him Karl Marx) tried to tack down "intrinsic values" above and beyond market values in order to insist that some things (e.g., human labor) had their true worth even if certain commodities were left to the vicissitudes of supply and demand.

What counts as fair, accordingly, is always in some sense a

subjective judgment, based not just on the individual feelings and needs of the immediate participants but on the larger collective consciousness as well. Fairness in business, in particular, is a certain kind of attunement, a willingness to exchange value for value in a market that provides no ultimately objective guideposts. It also means that negotiation is essential to business. We are misled by the fact that most of the goods and services we buy are offered to us with a price tag, as if the value were already concluded (which we notice, especially when prices are set too high). But the nature of the free market is that even the most "set" prices are the outcome of implicit negotiation, namely the anticipation of what customers will or will not pay, and what they will or will not buy. The centrality of negotiation is more evident in those markets where the very idea of a fixed price is nonsensical (e.g., securities markets, Moroccan bazaars). Fairness in the market is a function of mutual agreement, and nothing violates our sense of fairness so much as the violation of those (explicit or implicit) agreements.

Generosity

Context: you have, the others have not
Basic Concern(s): sharing, the well-being of others
Myth: the original Saint Nicholas
Useful to Self: sense of positive impact on others, satisfaction with one's own largesse
Useful to Others: meeting their needs, surpassing their expectations
Excess: giving away the store
Deficiency: miserliness (Scrooge)
Acid Test: Are you willing to give your valuable time, not only money, to those who really need it?

Generosity is too often thought to be the overcoming of miserliness, that is, wrestling with one's more selfish impulses. But, at least sometimes, the less wrestling one does, the more generous one is. Generosity may be compromised, rather than enhanced, by excessive deliberation. Generosity is exemplary among the virtues in that the more it is a cultivated, even "unthinking" habit, the more virtuous it may be. Compare the person who wrestles with his or her cheapness to someone whose generosity flows unthinkingly, as water flows from a fountain. The latter need not act on any sense of principle or obligation. He or she may give no thought at all to what he or she can afford to give. Would not we say that the more generous act is that which is spontaneous rather than forced? This is not to say that one ought to "give away the store," but that generosity, as a virtue, is not somethng forced or against one's own self-interest.

Graciousness

Context: interactions with other people
Basic Concern(s): establishing and maintaining an environment of congeniality and elegance
Myth: Cary Grant, Jackie O.
Useful to Self: sense of competence, control, and self-esteem
Useful to Others: a comfortable, charming, relaxing situation
Excess: unctuousness, fussiness
Deficiency: boorishness, haughtiness, tactlessness
Acid Test: Dealing with the competition when you're losing badly, or winning; dealing with troublesome customers.

Graciousness would seem more like a virtue for garden party hosts and hostesses than for businesspeople, but this, perhaps, is also part of the negative image long connected with business life. But there is nothing in the nature of business that excludes elegance, and if the excuse is that "it costs too much," that points not so much to tight budgets as to lack of imagination. As high-end retailers (and bankers, lawyers, and professionals in general) know, grace and elegance are extremely marketable, if not as commodities, then as environment. But graciousness does not just (or primarily) refer to elegance of presentation. It first and foremost points to a way of being in the world, a way of dealing with other people—confidently, generously, and with understanding.

Gratitude (see *Humility*)

Heroism

Context: courage under fire
Basic Concern(s): to do the right thing in the face of tremendous obstacles
Myth: Hercules, J. Burke of Johnson & Johnson in the Tylenol tragedy
Useful to Self: not feeling at the mercy of events, fullest self-realization, the admiration of others
Useful to Others: someone to emulate, a role model and a leader, inspiration
Excess: recklessness, self aggrandizement
Deficiency: overcaution, excess ego (but heroism is by its very nature above and beyond the call of duty ["supererogatory"], so failure to be a hero is not itself a vice)
Acid Test: Your code of ethics declares that you will act one way. Your financial well-being dictates the opposite. (Burke of Johnson & Johnson: "Given our promise to take care of the customer, there was nothing else we could do, nothing.")

Byron, in his epic poem *Don Juan*, wrote, "I want a hero, an uncommon want / When every year and month sends forth a new one." We understand all too easily the nature of that complaint. The business world is filled with temporary heroes, but it lacks someone who can really endure being looked up to. Lee Iacocca held the treasured status for several years after he saved Chrysler, until he tried to sabotage and buy back the company. Investment guru Warren Buffet is a populist candidate today, although, unfortunately, he is admired more for being one of the richest men in America than for his admirable scruples and modesty.

One might ask, quite reasonably, whether we should really want or need heroes. (Our heroes in this society tend to be professional athletes and movie stars, rarely moral heroes.) Do heroes interfere with our own autonomy or blunt our moral sensibilities? The latter is true only if we choose the wrong heroes. The former is true only if we expect our heroes to do all of the work and make the tough choices while we remain out of the loop ourselves. But heroes are human, after all, and all too often we expect, most unreasonably, that those who take on the most difficult and challenging roles in our society will be without flaws or blemishes.

We choose our heroes, and that choice is a reflection of our values. Our heroes show us the path that we ourselves want to follow, and we keep these ideals tangibly before us. They represent what we want to be, or wish we could be. So what does it say of us that we are so absorbed with the rich and famous, the merely good-looking, and the (fictional) roles they play, and those sometimes very rude sports stars? What does it say, then, *not* to have heroes? In *Corporate Cultures*, Deal and Kennedy say that "heroism is a leadership component that is all but forgotten by modern management. Since the 1920s, the corporate world has been powered by managers who are rationalists, who do strategic planning, write memos and devise flow charts. . . . Managers run institutions; heroes create them."[72]

Honesty

Context: any context in which the truth is called for

Basic Concern(s): to tell the truth, not to lie (these are not the same)

Myth: The apocryphal George Washington: "I cannot tell a lie."

Useful to Self: makes it easy to keep your stories straight, not having to cover up, making it more likely that you will be believed the next time, establishing trust and candor

Useful to Others: confidence in knowing, trusting, being able to believe; no need for suspicion

Excess: honest to a fault; telling the truth even when it is uncalled for, when it hurts, to the wrong person, oblivious to the larger context

Deficiency: liar, liar

Acid Test: Your client asks you if you have the brand that you're selling. (You don't. You have the competitor's version.)

Honesty is the first virtue of business life. Honesty, sweet and simple, means telling the truth, being told what you are getting, or, at least, what you are letting yourself in for. Honesty does not, however, mean full disclosure, and there are certain aspects of every transaction that are expected to be unknown and undisclosed. Every transaction involves a certain amount of risk and uncertainty, and that risk and uncertainty may even be the focus of the deal itself (as in certain forms of gambling and, of course, in securities exchanges). If someone buys a used car or an old house, he or she cannot possibly be expected to be told everything about the liabilities about to be obtained. Indeed, the practice of buying used cars (and to a lesser extent old houses) is already riddled with high expectations about risk and low expectations about disclosure.

A seller may not tell about a shaky transmission or a potentially leaky roof, but he or she is bound to tell the truth if asked. (The Roman philosopher Cicero worried about leaky roofs two thousand years ago, and where roofs are involved, business ethics seems not to have changed much since then.) Not knowing the answer to a direct question may sometimes be an excuse for not answering, but not always. There are some things that the buyer can be expected to ask and has the right to know, which means the seller has an obligation to find out in turn. (A record of automobile mileage, for example, is tightly regulated by law, and a house check for termite infestation is now built into mandated purchase agreements in most states in the United States) "Good faith" provisions often dictate what is relevant to a business transaction, but it would be a mistake to think of these as spelled out explicitly, much less formulated into law.

Not disclosing is different from a refusal to disclose, and this is different again from dishonesty. As so often occurs in matters of ethics, when distinctions are made in black and white, an adequate understanding is closed to us.[73] The contrast between honesty and dishonesty is not a simple "black-and-white" contrast between right and wrong, but (to extend the metaphor) they are two extremes in a rich colorful spectrum, in which the presence of risk and uncertainty as well as the frequent need to not "tell all" render both black and white a painterly and often illusory surface of many mixed colors. Insofar as every transaction involves some risk, it also precludes total honesty, even the seemingly straightforward "I don't know."

Sometimes, not disclosing means simply not having been asked the right question ("You never asked me"), but sometimes the question can be taken for granted, even if never thought of ("Well, you never asked me if the automobile had an engine").

Refusal to disclose when asked is not necessarily unethical, but it certainly changes the nature of the transaction. There is also the *right* to know. Business (like much else in life) may involve bluffing, but ordinary business presumes candor and straightforward information.

Honor (Pride)

Context: any situation in which one's self-respect is at stake
Basic Concern(s): to "hold one's head up high," to represent the good
Myth: Lucretia, the Roman wife who would rather die than lose her honor
Useful to Self: maintaining self-respect
Useful to Others: someone to respect, admire, trust
Excess: self-righteousness, snobbishness, obstinacy
Deficiency: self-debasement, lack of scruples, lack of virtue
Acid Test: What, in your job, would you absolutely refuse to do? (Suppose your boss asked you to lie to your best customer?)

Honor is a "supervirtue" in that it embraces virtually all of the others. Thus honor is often used as a (somewhat antiquated) synonym for "integrity." Aristotle used it in a more limited sense, to refer to one's public status only. As we are using it here, the word refers both to one's public status and to one's view of one's self, "in one's own eyes." In a more modern sense, we might think of honor as self-respect (as opposed to more personal self-esteem). "Honor" means "pride," which is one of the "seven deadly sins," but it is in fact a necessary virtue (it does not mean "vanity"—a very different and hardly virtuous emotion).[74] Pride is a highly individual emotion, but it is also a deeply social emotion, having to do with our standing (and our own perception of our standing) with others. (When people say that they are defending their honor but in fact are only nursing their personal pride, we find such behavior not only foolish but pretentious as well.)

Honor requires a sense of belonging, a sense of membership, a sense of self that is inseparable from one's group identity. It is only in the exceptional (and usually tragic) case that one's sense of self is anti-social, in opposition to others only. Honor involves living up to the expectations of the group—whether these are spelled out as a code of honor or a set of moral rules or simply implicit in the practices and goals of the group. One's honor, in other words, is rarely or never one's honor alone. It is the honor of the community or the corporation that one represents. In business, this sense of honor is an ancient virtue that might well be put to good modern use. It helps clarify both the role of the individual employee or executive in the corporation and all of our roles in society. Honor is not opposed to success and profitability. Indeed there is no success without it, and not much likelihood of continued profits either.

The other side of honor is shame, a vital social emotion. In our society, there is the idea that one's main objective after public humiliation is to "get over it." This idea undermines the seriousness of a sense of honor. While we need not endorse the old notions of exile and banishment (although a few convicted security fraud felons have so suffered), it is perhaps a social liability that we no longer take seriously the concept of a "ruined life." Today, one just declares bankruptcy or quits and moves to another town or gets another job or sets up another company and starts over. But in practical terms, what this means is that the business community is notoriously poor in sanctioning its own policies and punishing even the most flagrant offenders of its own rules. A restoration of the sense of honor would thus make a big difference in the contemporary business climate.

Humility

Context: situations of success and achievement
Basic Concern(s): not to think too highly of yourself, to give proper credit to others where credit is due
Myth: "I couldn't have done it without you."
Useful to Self: realistic expectations of self, a rewarding sense of gratitude, avoids the pitfalls of *chutzpah*
Useful to Others: sharing, less threatening, credit where credit is due

Excess: self-mortification, humiliation
Deficiency: arrogance, false pride, overbearingness, *chutzpah*
Acid Test: Your big success, high praise from the boss, your team lost from view in the shadows (consider the typical Academy Award speech).

David Hume called humility "the monkish virtue" and contrasted it with pride. Pride, of course, is one of the seven deadly sins, and Hume was making a polemical point, that pride is good and necessary (see **Honor**) and humility can sometimes be pathetic. But humility does not have to be pathetic; it is often no more than a realistic assessment of one's own contribution and the recognition of the contribution of others, along with luck and good fortune, that made one's own success possible. Humility, accordingly is a version of **gratitude**, another neglected virtue in business.

Humor

Context: both when there is something to laugh about and, sometimes, when there seems not to be something to laugh about
Basic Concern(s): to bring relief, to make the world a "lighter" place, to get a certain distance on ourselves and our serious pursuits
Myth: ideally, laughing at oneself (e.g., Walter Huston at the end of the movie *Treasure of the Sierra Madre* belly-laughing as his hard-earned fortune in gold dust blows away)
Useful to Self: lightens the world, intrinsically enjoyable
Useful to Others: lightens the world, intrinsically enjoyable
Excess: no sense of seriousness, humor that is "over the line," not knowing when not to laugh
Deficiency: no sense of humor, taking everything literally, being a sourpuss, being unable to laugh at oneself, not knowing when to laugh
Acid Test: You catch your tie in the paper shredder, in front of everyone.

It is worth noting that the virtue of having a sense of humor does not often appear on lists of virtues, despite the fact that in virtually every age and every culture, it has been recognized as an essential feature of human life. The importance of a sense of humor is nowhere more essential than in the modern corporation. For example, one of the most important characters in any organization is the person whom we might well call the "clown." An organization entirely composed of clowns would be dysfunctional, to say the least,[75] but one person with an exceptional sense of humor makes work much more enjoyable. It can make the company more flexible and resilient too.

Independence ("the Outlaw")

Context: any coherent group or organizational context
Basic Concern(s): to get things done, despite the bureaucracy and "little minds"
Myth: Robin Hood, Rambo, "the outlaw"
Useful to Self: self-confidence and self-satisfaction
Useful to Others: someone who will, if not lead the way, at least get things done
Excess: organizational destructiveness, extreme arrogance, antisocial behavior
Deficiency: being like everyone else, "going along with the crowd"
Acid Test: "You're fired if you do that!"

In their book *Corporate Cultures*, Deal and Kennedy celebrated a curious corporate hero whom they called "the outlaw," someone who flaunts the rules but, nevertheless, is an admirable and exemplary employee:

Perhaps no other situational hero fires the imagination of employees more than the outlaw or maverick: Billy the Kid, Patton, bad boys with a heart of gold. This hero is necessary when the company needs some degree of creativity for a challenge to existing values. Outlaws can symbolize the darker side of an organization, yet their bizarre behavior will release the pent-up tension everyone feels.[76]

The occasional contradiction between virtues and moral rules, between the more ordinary virtues and the extraordinary virtues of saints, heroes, and geniuses, helps to explain the ethical phenomenon of the outlaw or, as we might say without that hint of criminality, rebellious independence of thought and action. Robin Hood is perhaps the outstanding (English-speaking) example. Rambo is a more recent (and more dubious) example. Outlaws are familiar heroes and heroines in contemporary American literature and culture, even if they are too often ignored in ethics as such. In the movies, the outlaw character (usually played by a charming figure, Burt Reynolds or Goldie Hawn, for example) is at odds with the law but with a good heart and for a good cause. In corporate America, questionable corporate policies or procedures are more likely to be at stake. The outlaw, within the bounds of legality, nevertheless shows how far the bounds of propriety may be creatively challenged.

Why should such a "virtue" be mentioned in business ethics at all, except perhaps as an unfortunate popular example of rampant immorality? Because, first of all, like it or not, these are the "heroes" and "heroines" who now provide the moral examples for millions of Americans, executives as well as children. Second, such examples illustrate quite clearly the complexity of our actual morals and moral conceptions, which are not limited to universal rules and obedience but, quite the contrary, include a distinctive admiration for those who dare to be different—so long as they are sufficiently charming, productive, and, need we say, virtuous in other regards.

Integrity

Context: alone or with others, in any circumstances
Basic Concern(s): to be one's true (good) self
Myth: the incorruptible, "The Untouchables" (Eliot Ness, that is), the self-contained "whole person"
Useful to Self: only with integrity does one truly have a self
Useful to Others: a model of trustworthiness, dependability, virtue
Excess: (no such thing, though obstinacy is sometimes confused with integrity)
Deficiency: the failure of one or more of the key virtues

Acid Test: Your life fits together as a coherent, virtuous whole.

(See Part II, "The Meaning of Integrity" pp. 38–40.)

Justice

Context: any situation in which there are goods (or punishments) to be distributed
Basic Concern(s): to give everyone their due, whether reward or punishment
Myth: the righteous are rewarded; the wicked are punished
Useful to Self: to be treated fairly
Useful to Others: that they are treated fairly
Excess: when justice utterly eclipses compassion and utility
Deficiency: injustice, favoritism, greed, vengefulness
Acid Test: Two employees just screwed up. One of them is a friend and very productive. The other is a new recruit and a bit annoying. But what they did wrong is exactly the same.

Justice in business is part of a tradition that precedes by many centuries business life as we know it. It goes back to the ancient Aristotelian and medieval conception of the "just wage" and the "fair price" and the more abstract "labor theory of value" that was embraced by both Adam Smith and Karl Marx. More recently, the philosopher John Rawls has written, "Justice is the first virtue of social institutions, as truth is of systems of thought."[77] Business, and corporations more particularly, are social institutions, and justice, which Rawls interprets as "fairness," if it is not the first virtue, is, at any rate, one of the most essential business virtues. But Robert Townsend, former CEO of Avis and author of *Up the Organization*, writes, "Fairness, justice, whatever you call it—it's essential and most companies don't have it."[78] Indeed, a great many companies seem to be built on principles of injustice and unfairness, and this is not just an ethical concern. Injustice and lack of fairness breed resentment and poison in the workforce.

Aristotle lists justice as one of his basic virtues—indeed, he sometimes suggests (as did Plato) that it is *the* basic virtue—but he has in mind the idea of justice not as an abstract scheme but rather as a personal virtue. The good person, especially the good administrator, has the right "sense" of justice, that is, he or she "sees" what is just and fair. In the corporation, justice is not only a virtue but an utter necessity. People "see" quite clearly whether what is being done is just or not, and how they behave—what they are willing to give to the company—is determined more by this than by anything else.

Nevertheless, justice has a variety of meanings; indeed, "what is justice?" is one of the oldest questions in social philosophy.[79] Some, like Rawls, think of justice as fairness, as everyone getting their fair share and giving everyone an opportunity. Some thinkers insist that justice has only to do with outcomes, whereas others insist that justice means following the right procedures, even if the outcome, on occasion, is undesirable. Some say that justice is reward (or punishment) according to merit or luck, and others insist that "everyone ought to get what they need." Then, again, a good deal of justice, for example, *compensatory justice* and *retributive justice*, have more to do with the righting of wrongs or the punishment of wrongdoing.

A shared sense of justice holds an organization together. Injustice, by contrast, sets up envious and bitter relationships and sets people against one another. As fairness, it is the fact and perception that everyone in (and connected with) the organization is getting their due. In particular, this means that people get recognized for what they do and are properly rewarded with commendations, bonuses, and promotions; that people are hired into positions they deserve and given duties commensurable with their abilities and salary; and, of course, that they are paid and paid on time. The bond between the individual and the organization cannot be maintained on the basis of loyalty alone, nor can it be understood as a merely contractual arrangement. It is a bond that involves a presumption of justice, the demand that one is recognized and respected for what one is, that one is not neglected or "shortchanged," that one is not exploited or abused. This requires diligence on the part of the corporation, since one can be sure that the individual employee or manager will be. Nothing fosters resentment faster than the perception that one is being paid less or given less recognition for his or her accomplishments than someone else, and nothing fosters negative competition more readily than the perception that someone else is getting the rewards that one oneself deserves.

It has recently been suggested that what is missing from the standard views of justice is an adequate sense of care and compassion. This is, I believe, true and important. John Rawls, whose liberal credentials and sense of compassion are not in question, finds it necessary to dress his sentiments in the formal costume of an impersonal deduction of rational principles, and most of the literature that has followed him has shown far more enthusiasm for his form than for his feelings. Justice is, first of all, a sense of compassion. But this is not an "either/or" situation—impersonal justice *or* personal concern. The kindly sentiments represented by care and compassion cannot by themselves explain the enormous range or the systematic nature of the passions that constitute our sense of justice, including our often vehement and not at all kindly sense of injustice. Sentiments alone cannot solve or account for the large policy issues that are (or should be) the ultimate concern of justice, but a sense of justice nevertheless begins with them.

Loyalty

Context: membership in any organization

Basic Concern(s): the well-being of the organization and the status of one's membership in it

Myth: "My only regret is that I have but one life to give for my country."

Useful to Self: a sense of belonging (and loyalty in return)

Useful to Others: a sense of trust and affection, superseding self interest

Excess: blind loyalty, refusal to be critical or to see the larger picture, fanaticism

Deficiency: disloyalty, "on sale to the highest bidder," treachery, betrayal

Acid Test: Do you fully support the organization even when you don't get the promotion you deserve?

Loyalty is one of those virtues that—with the rise of radical individualism, a loss of the sense of virtue, the emphasis on policies and principles to the neglect of the person—had all but dropped out of business ethics. Or it was simply taken for granted as an enduring feature of corporate membership. But now, with downsizing and rapid turnover in companies, loyalty is seriously under fire. Indeed, some pundits have argued that loyalty is a thing of the past. Now there are only contracts and "employment at will." This is unthinkable. No organization can long endure without the loyalty of its members. Desperation and coercion, perhaps a temporary challenge, might effectively hold people in place for a short amount of time. But loyalty is nothing less than that set of affections that makes people care about what they are doing and for whom they are doing it. Without loyalty, a corporation is just a tentative collection of people temporarily allied in a project that, more often than not, means very little to them. Loyalty is as essential to a successful corporation as brand name is to a successful product.

Business ethics has often ignored loyalty in favor of the more abstract and universal concept of "rights." So long as we respect contracts, the discussion goes, what is the point of a superfluous and perhaps childish emotion like loyalty? Of course, loyalty (like patriotism, one special variant of it) can be a refuge from responsibility or a forum for venal self-righteousness, but it does not follow—as many people seem to think it does—that it is an emotion that has lost its place in the corporate world. But there are different levels of loyalty—to the organization as a whole, to the department, to the product, to one's boss, to the values of the corporation. One must also be loyal to one's conscience, to one's own values, to the standards of one's profession. Loyalty to the company's values or to the standards of one's profession, for example, may occasionally require breaking ranks with one's boss. (Here, in particular, is where loyalty and integrity painfully meet.)

Against the recent "work-for-hire" approach to employer-employee relations, I would want to argue that an emphasis on loyalty—and that means loyalty in *both* directions—has a lot to offer to business ethics that too often gets dismissed with the usual stories of uncritical loyalty and gross corporate malfeasance. Alexander B. Horniman has recently written:

The concept of loyalty has changed from one of "blind and

obligated" to one of "insightful and earned." . . . Loyalty tends to be more easily earned in those organizations that have clearly-defined values and challenging standards. People are likely to be loyal to values that lead to outstanding achievements in products, services and relationships.[80]

Passion

Context: any task, project, engagement, relationship
Basic Concern(s): to engage the world with enthusiasm
Myth: "the grand passion," the love of one's life
Useful to Self: to live life to the fullest, to give one's all
Useful to Others: it is infectious, inspiring, and it gets
    things done
Excess: insanity, overzealousness, obnoxiousness
Deficiency: apathy, indifference, lack of motivation,
    uninspired, uninspiring
Acid Test: Can you continue to be passionately committed
    when everyone around you is tired and frustrated?

So much emphasis in business is placed on such notions as economic rationality that a whole dimension of business life gets ignored. Business is exciting, it is challenging, it is something that people love doing. Rationality may provide the guidelines of business activity, but it is passion that motivates it. That a salesperson is passionate about the product is not only good salesmanship. It gives meaning to what he or she is doing in life.

Pride (see *Honor*)

Prudence

Context: all actions or situations in which one has interests
    or vulnerabilities
Basic Concern(s): minimize personal (and company) losses
Myth: "look before you leap" (i.e., do a feasibility study, get
    background references, consider a worst-case scenario)
Useful to Self: essential to avoiding disaster (unless you are
    very, very lucky)

Useful to Others: confidence that you will avoid disaster
Excess: timidity, overly risk-aversive, compulsiveness, selfishness
Deficiency: recklessness, impulsiveness, risking others' interests as well
Acid Test: Cold call: "I've got a stock, an initial offering in an Asian gold mine, should be a hundred-bagger within ten months. But I've got to know right away."

Prudence is tied to self-interest, but it should not be confused with selfishness, one of its opposed vices. Prudence is looking out for yourself (or your family, your group, your company) and being careful, but it does not imply excessive self-interest nor does it suggest (in fact, it discourages) lack of interest or consideration in others' well-being. As a cardinal virtue, for example, in Christian theology, prudence required a certain humility and, as in Socrates' philosophy, the care and concern for one's "soul" by way of doing right and being virtuous.

Responsibility

Context: virtually all contexts, but especially any position in which you are or ought to be accountable
Basic Concern(s): to do what one can/ought to do, to make things right, to be accountable
Myth: Atlas, with the world on his shoulders
Useful to Self: knowing who you are (a person is defined, in part, by his or her responsibilities), getting things done, being honest with oneself and others
Useful to Others: knowing who is in charge of what, knowing that what is important will be done
Excess: taking on too much, taking responsibility for that which one could not possibly have acted upon or where one could not possibly be held accountable
Deficiency: taking on too little; making excuses; Ambrose Bierce: "responsibility, n. a detachable burden easily shifted to the shoulders of God, Fate or Fortune, or one's neighbor" (*The Devil's Dictionary*)

Acid Test: Take the blame when things go wrong. (Everyone is happy to take responsibility when things go well.)

A book could be written about responsibility as a personal virtue, but too few of our leaders would read it. Responsibility is confused with power and status, but it is, first of all, being in charge and being accountable. The dominant philosophy of our times, however, seems to be "cover your butt," in other words, evade, excuse, and deny responsibility. Responsibility is too often excluded from the list of virtues because it is considered not so much a personal trait as something more abstract that attaches to positions (a "position of responsibility," "part of my job is to x") or situations ("she was the one who was in contact with him, so she . . . "). Thus every middle manager knows the nightmare of being delegated responsibility without the authority or resources to see it through. But responsibility is also an essential trait of character, not only in business but in any enterprise or activity where something matters. Some people tend, by habit, by training, by temperament, to accept responsibility. Others do not. The latter should never be put into "positions of responsibility," but, all too often, they are. This is the danger of *not* thinking about responsibility first of all as an essential trait of character, a personal virtue, and not just something that one "picks up" with the job.

Saintliness

Context: ordinary human situations, extraordinary behavior
Basic Concern(s): to be as "pure," as good, as close to ideal as possible
Myth: Saint Francis, Mother Teresa, Gandhi, the Buddha
Useful to Self: saintliness is its own reward (it has to be)
Useful to Others: as an inspiration, as an ideal (sometimes productive)
Excess: unworldliness
Deficiency: ordinary flaws and vices (but saintliness, like heroism, is supererogatory, above and beyond the call of duty)
Acid Test: The righteous whistle-blower (who, with any sense, knows that this will virtually never work out to his or her advantage).

Peter Drucker's comment is pertinent here: "If saints sat on the Board of Directors they would still have to worry about dividends." But, then again, it would be a pretty darn good company.

Shame (a "quasi-virtue")

Context: having done wrong
Basic Concern(s): regaining the acceptance of the group
Myth: Ivan Boesky, now studying the Talmud
Useful to Self: reaffirms group affiliation and a sense of responsibility
Useful to Others: reaffirms group solidarity and values
Excess: pathological guilt, withdrawal
Deficiency: shamelessness, unscrupulousness
Acid Test: No one knows you've done it, but . . .

Shame is a particularly painful emotion, but it is also an essential ingredient in ethics. Sociologist Thomas Scheff calls it "the emotional pivot of social life" and "a basic mechanism of social control." Aristotle awkwardly introduces it as a "quasi-virtue." The point is not that it is desirable to be ashamed, of course, but rather that the capacity for shame is essential to having a virtuous character. As the Ethiopian proverb goes, "Where there is no shame, there is no honor." Shame is a distinctively social emotion. It means that you let down your colleagues and others who trusted or depended on you. Thus John Rawls is right in part when he insists that shame is the opposite of self-esteem, since honor can be the criterion for self-esteem.[81] To feel shame (not quite the same as our "being ashamed") is quite literally to fail oneself, but in the context of one's larger, social self.

Not feeling shame may be the most offensive evidence of unethical attitudes and the lack of virtue. When a $100 million settlement was denied to Exxon for the *Valdez* disaster by a judge who rightly suspected that such an amount would be no more than the usual "cost of doing business" for the giant oil company, it was in answer to chairman Lawrence Rawl's announcement the preceding week to Exxon stockholders that the *Valdez* disaster "will not have a significant effect on our earnings." After the judge's action, *Newsweek* commented, "it may be the world's biggest oil company, but Exxon could learn a trick or two from a common street criminal: if there's one thing a judge wants to see when a miscreant makes a plea, it's remorse."[82]

Shame is often confused with guilt. Guilt is also an important moral emotion, but the capacity for guilt is not a virtue as the capacity for shame is. Guilt is often conflated with legal guilt, which is rather a different topic, and with neurotic, unjustified guilt (discussed at length by Freud, for example). Shame also has its pathological exaggerations, but in itself it is usually a justified and desirable response to one's own unethical behavior. (Gabrielle Taylor even argues that genuine shame is always justified.[83]) Guilt, on the other hand, has acquired an intriguing connection with religion (especially in Judaism and Christianity). Guilt also tends to be a more individualistic emotion. (Thus Christian guilt and sin are typically construed as guilt before God, not other people.)

Anthropologists often distinguish between guilt and shame societies, namely, those that are more tribal or communal and those that place more emphasis on the individual. (It is important not to infer from this distinction that shame societies are more primitive. Japanese culture, for instance, is paradigmatically a shame society. So was Aristotle's Athens.) Corporations might well be conceived as shame societies. They are (more or less) tight-knit communities with a shared identity, shared values, and common interests.

Although shame refers to the judgments of others, it is actually one's own self-condemnation reflecting the perceived or expected condemnation of others. In this, shame is extremely self-conscious as well as social. Thus the French existentialist Jean-Paul Sartre emphasizes "the look" of shame, the piercing gaze of others that "pins us down" for our transgressions. Yet shame remains first of all self-reflective, a form of self-condemnation, and in this we recognize, as Aristotle did, its status as a "quasi-virtue."

It is a "quasi-virtue" in that one may have done wrong but one at least takes the blame for what one has done and thus admits responsibility. One might try to avoid or deny this responsibility by insisting that one's actions were only foolish or incompetent (or, of course, blame one's behavior on others), but we can thus appreciate the virtue of shame. Shame is an emotion that presupposes a sense of responsibility. It also presupposes the importance of the group and assumes the validity of corporate or community values. Thus Aristotle rightly recognized its essential importance in any ethical community or corporation.

Spirit (Spirituality)

Context: ideally, in all matters (and, of course, all matters spiritual)
Basic Concern(s): the larger picture, the world beyond our practical concerns
Myth: all of the religions of the world, the world as One (not "the holy dollar")
Useful to Self: expansive, cosmically edifying
Useful to Others: something essentially shared
Excess: out-of-this-worldliness, self-righteousness, prejudice
Deficiency: vulgarity, materialism and self-interest
Acid Test: Would you consider a profound religious experience an interruption of your workday?

Spirit often refers merely to "energy," and *spirited* just means "lively." But *spirit* also refers to that larger aspect of us—of all of us—and the world viewed as something other than the nuts-and-bolts nature of science and a vast (if limited) realm of resources. *Spirituality* is often identified with religion, quite understandably, but it should not be identified with any particular religion or, for that matter, with only those religions that are organized as such. Spirituality embraces all sorts of personal cosmic outlooks. It embraces environmentalism in the large sense (that is, not just saving resources but an appreciation of Nature). It embraces a good deal of aesthetic appreciation (for example, all great music is spiritual). And it embraces a good deal of what still can be called "the love of humanity." What could be more irrelevant to business, you might ask? But the very opposite is true. Business, like spirituality (and virtually every other human endeavor), functions best when it has the most perspective, the larger outlook, vision beyond its immediate procedures and goals. It is no accident, looking back over the past several years, that a great many books on business borrow their most profound insights from religion, including such unbusinesslike philosophies as Buddhism and Taoism.

Style

Context: ideally, every facet of personal behavior

Basic Concern(s): to be interesting, elegant, even beautiful

Myth: the swashbuckling entrepreneur, Cary Grant, Kate Hepburn

Useful to Self: charm, elegance, attractiveness, memorability

Useful to Others: charming to them, lends elegance to every encounter (which, like inelegance, tends to be contagious)

Excess: foppishness, narcissism, neglect of more mundane tasks and projects

Deficiency: slovenliness, vulgarity, unintentioned ugliness

Acid Test: It's casual day, but the CEO is coming.

Nietzsche, in one of his best lines, tells us to "Give style to your character, a great art." Style is one of what we might call the Aesthetic Virtues, virtues that may not pertain directly to morality, congeniality, and efficiency but nevertheless may make the difference between a wonderful life and a life of indifferent worth—so, too, in an organization. Working for a company may be a source of great personal pride, or it can be an embarrassment, and in addition to the usual moral and economic factors, aesthetic considerations certainly play a role. "Style" should not be confused with "fashion," which is merely a matter of "keeping up," nor with having expensive tastes, which is quite compatible with the most atrocious taste and sensibilities. Style is not merely superficial but should be thought of as a deep expression of who a person really is, or, rather an expression of what is deepest about them. The complaint is often made that organizational style ("the corporate uniform") is antithetical to any real sense of style, but, perhaps, the opposite is true. As the great (and very stylish) poet Goethe used to say, the test is "freedom within limitation." What an artist can say with a limited palette is often more expressive (and impressive) than what can be said with an infinite array of paints. And, in any case, style is hardly just a question of what one wears. It is how one speaks, what one says, how one acts, how one thinks, how one feels. As the best CEOs and salespeople will readily tell you, along with the greatest artists and bon vivants of history, style is what really counts. As Robert Frost famously wrote, "Style is the man" (and the woman, too).

Tolerance

Context: any contact with other people, other habits, other ideas, other ways of doing things
Basic Concern(s): getting along
Myth: the peaceable kingdom (though let's not ask what the lions eat)
Useful to Self: peace, and being tolerated in return
Useful to Others: peace, and being tolerated in return
Excess: mushmindedness, lack of critical acumen, loss of standards
Deficiency: close-mindedness, ignorance, mean-spiritedness, unwarranted self-righteousness, mutual hostility
Acid Test: Someone tells a "politically incorrect" joke in your presence.

Is any virtue more essential than tolerance, in this multicultural, pluralistic society? There are many ways of doing things, and many things to learn. But this is not to say that one should always "do in Rome as the Romans do," nor is it an excuse for lack of guts, lack of integrity, or a refusal to stand behind one's beliefs and values. Tolerance (like a great many virtues) is first of all good judgment, being able to see and think clearly what is merely different and what is truly offensive or a violation of one's ethics. This leads to a second order of tolerance, namely tolerance of one's own limits of tolerance, and a continuous questioning of one's rigidity.

Toughness

Context: any position of authority or responsibility
Basic Concern(s): to maintain one's position, to get things done

Myth: George Washington, George Patton, Golda Meir, not Simon Legree of *Uncle Tom's Cabin*, who was cruel and ruthless
Useful to Self: effective, impressive, good for self-esteem and self-respect
Useful to Others: knowing where they stand, and that someone will take charge and see it through
Excess: cruelty, obstinacy, ruthlessness, thick-headedness
Deficiency: passivity, weakness, lack of backbone
Acid Test: When someone even more powerful (but wrong) stands up to you.

Toughness is perhaps the most misunderstood virtue in business life. The word "tough" is typically used by way of admiration, though often coupled with a shake of the head and an expression of frustration. Sometimes it is used as a euphemism, in place of or in conjunction with various synonyms for a nasty or odious human being. Not infrequently, it simply means stubborn, impossible, or mean-spirited. But toughness is generally and genuinely perceived as a virtue, albeit a virtue that is often misplaced and misconceived. Insofar as business consists of bargaining and dealing with other people, toughness is essential, and its opposite is not so much weakness as it is incompetence. But much of what is called toughness is neither a virtue nor a vice. It is not a character trait so much as it is a skill, whether cultivated or natural. In certain central business practices, notably negotiating, toughness is not so much a personal virtue as it is a technique or set of techniques, an acquired manner and an accomplished strategy, "knowing when to hold 'em, knowing when to fold 'em." Toughness includes knowing how to bluff and when to keep silent, when to be cooperative and when not to be. But such a skill is not unethical or divorced from ordinary morals; it is a legitimate part of a certain kind of obviously legitimate activity. Yet, as a specific skill or set of skills, being a tough negotiator is not sufficiently personal or general to count as a virtue, which is not to say, of course, that it is not therefore admirable or necessary.

Very often, what "toughness" means is simply "smart," that is, knowing the business, knowing one's competitors and dealings, knowing how to get things done. Again, this is an admirable and necessary set of business qualifications but not, as such, a virtue. But "toughness" also means "perseverance," which is a personal as well as a business virtue. As always, Aristotle's standard of moderation comes into play here, for there is such a thing as too much perseverance, which then becomes mere obstinacy or stubbornness. Of course, what seemed like obstinacy to those of little faith may well turn out to be richly rewarded by the results, and what was indeed healthy perseverance may nevertheless turn to failure in the vicissitudes of the market. But too little "stick-to-itiveness" makes success virtually impossible and makes life intolerable for those investors, employees, and other stakeholders who naturally depend on a full-blooded effort rather than a halfhearted try. Toughness as perseverance means nothing other than having a goal and a purpose, seeing its worthiness, and pursuing it to the end. What makes it "tough" is facing up to setbacks and obstacles that would discourage lesser beings; indeed, it is only in the face of failure that such toughness is truly tested, for it is no virtue to "persevere" when the market is handing you nothing but success.

Toughness in an executive also has an ethically painful element. Sometimes it is necessary to do something wrong in order to do what is right. Powerful politicians, of course, face such dilemmas all of the time, giving rise to a substantial literature on the controversial virtue of toughness and ruthlessness and the allegedly opposed domains of public and private morality.[84] Sometimes, to reach a higher goal, one must do what one otherwise would not and should not even consider. For example, in the face of debts or deficiencies that will very likely capsize the company, a chairman may need to let go perfectly qualified, hardworking, loyal employees. Viewed as an action isolated from the circumstances, letting people go for no reason whatever—that is, for no fault of their own—would be the height of injustice. But if it is a matter of saving the company, then this otherwise unjust act may nevertheless be necessary. Toughness is being able and willing to undertake such measures. This is not to say, however—and this cannot be emphasized enough—that such decisions can or should be made without guilt or pain or bad feelings. It does not mean that what one has done is not, despite its necessity, wrong. The chief executive of a large corporation once told me that downsizing his company was the most painful thing he had ever had to do. His toughness lay not in callousness or indifference but in his insistence on doing what was necessary as humanely as possible. Indeed, callousness and indifference are not themselves signs of toughness but the very opposite, indications of that form of weakness that can face moral issues only by denying them. Toughness is a virtue, but callousness and indifference are not, and they should never be confused.

Trust

Context: any interpersonal context or relationship
Basic Concern(s): to be able to depend on others
Myth: the ideal marriage, the perfect partnership
Useful to Self: allows delegation and dependency
Useful to Others: inspires trustworthiness and confidence
Excess: foolish trust, blind trust
Deficiency: inability to delegate, becoming closed, isolated, mistrustful, even paranoid
Acid Test: "Dad, may I use the car tonight?"

The word *trust* appears in virtually every book on business these days, and it is now taken as a commonplace that without trust, no business arrangement is possible. Francis Fukuyama, for example, has recently published a four-hundred-page book on the subject, entitled *Trust*.[85] But trust should not immediately be reduced to the level of contracts, legally drawn or merely "implicit," for trust precedes (and often obviates) the need for contracts. Indeed, contracts may indicate a lack of trust, and it is symptomatic of our current business climate that contracts have now become virtually universal, and even then, it is the "legal power to back them up" that is often taken as the ultimate sanction.

Several standard definitions of trust characterize it primarily in terms of *expectations*,[86] but this is only half of the story. It also involves decisions and the dynamics of a relationship. Niklas Luhmann distinguishes trust from confidence, noting that we trust (or don't trust) people but have (or do not have) confidence in institutions. I think this points to an important distinction, but it does not yet reach it. The distinction between persons and organizations is convenient and obvious, but often, especially in business and organizational ethics, this distinction is misleading or counterproductive. Organizations and institutions have many of the same features as people (not least, that in the eye of the law they are persons, with fiduciary obligations, rights, and responsibilities). As such, we trust them (or not), much as we would trust a person who had made us a promise or with whom we had a contractual agreement. On the other hand, we sometimes have confidence in people we do not or would not trust, for example, bureaucrats who are constrained by the law but are personally unknown to us. We may also have confidence in someone precisely because we do not trust them, for instance, when we place our confidence in the double-dealing habits of an old and well-known enemy or "have confidence" that our friend will fail to quit smoking this time as he has every one of the last thirty-one attempts to do so. (This use of "have confidence" is not wholly ironic.)

Trust, by contrast, is not just predicting that something will occur. Organizations and institutions are not mechanisms, no matter how efficiently they may be constructed. Organizations and institutions are people, working together. Relationships by their nature involve much more than a calculation of probabilities and outcomes. They involve values and emotions, responsibilities and the possibility of not only disappointment but betrayal. Thus trust is often a personal decision, whether to trust someone or not (however strong or weak the evidence for his or her trustworthiness). Trust, in other words, is dynamic. It is not merely a connective (the "glue" of relationships—Kenneth Arrow) or an "atmosphere" (Sisela Bok). Such talk tends to make trust get taken for granted. But as we all know from our own experience, whether or not to trust someone can be a very conscientious, difficult, and extremely important decision.

Trustworthiness

Context: any interpersonal context or relationship
Basic Concern(s): to be trusted, to fulfill one's responsibilities and to be seen to do so
Myth: Penelope, holding the fort and waiting patiently for her husband, Odysseus
Useful to Self: increases one's sense of responsibility, and leads to more responsibilities

Useful to Others: allows them to trust in confidence
Excess: none, really (although, in a tough negotiation, not
  being able to bluff can be a real disadvantage)
Deficiency: untrustworthiness, and no one will trust you;
  increased isolation, breeding distrust, causing paranoia
Acid Test: "May I leave the amount blank on this check I just
  signed?"

Trust must be distinguished from trustworthiness. Although "trust" is often treated as an umbrella term for the trusting relationship, there is a difference—an important difference—between trusting and being trusted (although in most relationships there is some of each in every direction). To be trustworthy is to be worthy of trust, to have earned the right to be trusted. One might be trusted even without being trustworthy (for example, in the case where no one else is available), but one certainly should not expect to be trusted without having established one's trustworthiness. And, without trust, one's future in business is or should be limited, to say the least. Business can tolerate a certain amount of cheating and irresponsibility at the margins, but, as an institution and a social practice, it is based on the premise that most people are trustworthy. They do what they say they will do. They pay when they say they will pay. They are who they say they are. The currency of the business world isn't money; it is trust and trustworthiness. Without money, we could all go back to the barter system (admittedly, with some inconvenience). But without trust and trustworthiness, one could not even barter. (Nor, of course, would there be any money, for what is money other than an intrinsically worthless piece of paper plus trust?)

Wittiness

Context: any situation that could use some levity
Basic Concern(s): to lighten conversation, to add a
  dimension of play, to display one's own cleverness to the
  enjoyment of others
Myth: a Monty Python office skit
Useful to Self: lightens the world, displays one's own
  cleverness, attracts attention

Useful to Others: lightens the world, enjoyable
Excess: silly and distracting, no sense of seriousness, not
  knowing when to shut up
Deficiency: taking everything too seriously
Acid Test: "A duck, a rabbit, and an undertaker walk into the
  New York Stock exchange and . . ."

Wittiness is not quite the same as having a sense of humor. For one thing, it is enough to have a sense of humor if one recognizes and appreciates what is funny, whereas wittiness is the capacity to actually *produce* humor. Not everyone has it, nor would it be a good thing if everyone did have it. It is much better that wit remains the spice, not the substance, of conversation. Nevertheless, it is a neglected virtue, one without which life would be much more bland and humorless than it is.

Zeal (Enthusiasm)

Context: anything really worth doing
Basic Concern(s): to make the most of any challenge, to
  get the job done
Myth: the phrase "gung ho!"
Useful to Self: makes life interesting, makes work
  meaningful
Useful to Others: enthusiasm is contagious
Excess: fanaticism, not knowing when to stop
Deficiency: "just doing my job"
Acid Test: Obstacles, criticism, cynicism: no matter.

Zeal is directed passion, enthusiasm applied. The difference between work and a mission is the meaningfulness of the latter and the zeal that accompanies it. All too often, discussions of ethics in business are restricted to the passionless necessity of rules and constraints, but what is equally (or more) important is the positive enthusiasm we have for meaningful tasks. What makes ethics essential to business is not just the need for restraint and social responsibility. It is also the inspiration and drive that make us believe in what we are doing.

Putting It All Together: Ethical Styles

Give style to your character, a great art.
—Friedrich Nietzsche

This partial but already bewildering survey of the virtues might well seem either overwhelming or overly formulaic. It may seem overwhelming in that there are so many virtues, all desirable, each of them to be cultivated. (Wouldn't it be easy if there were only one?) So how is a harried businessperson to make a start? The answer, of course, is that, with a decent upbringing and a few good friends, we started cultivating these virtues in childhood, and while each and every virtue has its own skills and significance, we tend to learn many of them together, a convenience Aristotle referred to as "the unity of the virtues."

As for being overly formulaic, this list and the two-part discussion that precedes it are not intended as a recipe for ethics. Indeed, that is the problem I encounter in so many ethics discussions, the expectation that a class or workshop in ethics will produce a hard-and-fast list of rules and instructions, to apply to whatever ethically sensitive situation comes along. But the whole point of the "Aristotelian" approach that I have presented here is to get away from this overly formulaic way of thinking about ethics and emphasize instead the very personal nature and the context-sensitivity of ethics. Our list of virtues may be general (which is not to deny that the list will vary considerably from culture to culture), but the virtues themselves are always individual. They belong to this person or that corporation. Nietzsche, who also wrote extensively on the virtues, suggests that each virtue is "unique," that your virtue is yours and unlike anyone else's.[87] I would not want to go so far, but I think the point is very important. We all have our own way of putting the virtues together and forging our own ethical characters. We all, in other words, have our own *ethical style*.

For many centuries, professional ethicists have competed against one another with their favorite ethical "theories," that is, their ideas about the basic principles or considerations that define ethics and ethical reasoning. Like most battles of this sort, this one never seems to end. New twists and turns are always emerging, and virtue ethics—as the approach I have presented here is sometimes called—has become one more contender for the status of *the correct* ethical theory. I believe that all of this is a waste of time and energy, not because the considerations are unimportant but rather because there can be no fixed answer to the question, What is most important in ethics? The idea that there are different ethical styles implies that, in practice, different theories will apply (more or less) to different ways of dealing ethically with the world. For some people, ethics really is and must be, as I noted at the very beginning of the book, a set of commandments imposed or "handed down" from above. For others, and I think for most people, ethics must include concerns for the well-being of others, a concern for fairness, a sense of coherence and consistency. But ethics also consists of the individual mix of virtues (and vices) that makes up each one of us and defines the perspective through which we plan and judge our actions and those of others.

Ethical styles is a phrase and an idea that would have been utterly unacceptable until a few years ago—except, perhaps, to Nietzsche and Oscar Wilde. It smacks of relativism. It suggests not only subjectivism (which at least can be "deep" and supported by extensive reasons and reasoning) but superficiality as well—ethics and ethical behavior as fashion, a matter of personality or, worse, a costume of thoughts and actions that may be put aside as easily as it can be put on. Of course, different ethical styles have very different advantages and disadvantages, and it may well be that an ethical style is no more easily changed than other lifelong traits of character such as thoughtfulness, recklessness, or spontaneous generosity. Nevertheless, the idea that the utilitarian and the Kantian are just expressing personal differences, rather than arguing once and for all about what is really "right," grates against our philosophical sensibilities. Is the "categorical imperative" (the absolute rule) really just a Kantian fashion, perhaps typical of certain personality types, and not the key to "morality" after all? Well, yes, but it must also be seen as the highlighting of some virtues rather than others, as an exemplary way of focusing the unity of one's virtues on whatever situation is at hand.

To say that there are different ethical styles is not to defend either relativism or subjectivism, it is not to say that "anything goes," and it is not to reduce ethics to fashion. But it is to emphasize—and celebrate—ethical differences. There are many ways of being ethical. Here are seven of them:

1. RULE-BOUND: thinking and acting on the basis of rules and principles, with only secondary regard to circumstances or possible exceptions.
2. UTILITARIAN: weighing probable consequences, both to the company or the profession and to the public well-being. Principles are important only as rules of thumb. "The greatest good for the greatest number of people" is the ultimate test for any action or decision.
3. PROFESSIONAL: evaluating all decisions first in terms of benefit to the profession, the institution, and the company and its reputation.
4. LOYALIST: duties and obligations defined by way of identification with the company or the organization. In business, "the company man."
5. VIRTUOUS: every action is measured in terms of its reflection on one's character (or the profession, institution, or company reputation) without immediate regard to consequences and often without paying much attention to general principles.
6. INTUITIVE: making decisions on the basis of conscience, even without deliberation, argument, or reasons. Intuitive thinkers tend to be impatient with more deliberative deontological and utilitarian types.
7. EMPATHETIC: following one's feelings of sympathy and compassion. "Putting oneself in the other's place" is the modus operandi of the empathetic style, whether the "other" be a competitor ("How would we like it if he . . .") or a client ("I can easily imagine how it would feel to be . . .").

The classic and most familiar clash of ethical styles is the sometimes bitter conflict between the rule-bound moralist and the utilitarian. The rule-bound moralist believes in the letter of the law.

(At meetings, he or she will very likely carry the policy handbook.) It may not even matter that the rule in question is outdated or impractical. It may not even matter that it became a matter of law or policy under another administration now out of office. It may not matter that the rule will no doubt be changed someday. The rule-bound moralist believes that one should obey rules, laws, regulations, and policies, whatever their origins and whatever the consequences. Any other way of thinking, from his or her standpoint, is amoral.

The utilitarian, on the other hand, is self-consciously practical. Rules serve a purpose, a function, and they are to be obeyed just because—but only because—they serve that purpose or function. A rule that proves to be impractical no longer deserves our respect or obedience. A rule that was formulated under very different circumstances or was legislated by a different administration should be carefully scrutinized and not given too much weight. The utilitarian makes his or her decisions on the sole ground that a certain course of action has the best consequences for everyone involved. If that fits the rules (as it usually does), then so much the better. If it does not, then so much the worse for the rules—and so much too for the rule-bound moralist, who because of sheer obstinacy or perhaps for some unfathomable personal reason refuses to see the point.

We know how this little scenario tends to go, from departmental meetings if not from arguments in ethics: The rule-bound moralist considers the utilitarian an opportunist, a "pragmatist," an amoral deviant, a man or woman who does not respect authority and the rules. The utilitarian considers the rule-bound moralist to be utterly unreasonable and impractical if not neurotic and "impossible." When general utility conflicts with an established rule, the utilitarian and the rule-bound moralist are sure to misunderstand one another. There can be no compromise because each of them considers his or her own position to be beyond negotiation, and neither can understand the other, except, perhaps, in the terms of moral pathology.

Ethical styles can go wrong. One way is to be inappropriate to the context. Whatever one's preferred style of thinking, there are contexts in which some styles are clearly appropriate, others clearly inappropriate. For example, speaking at a sales meeting, the rule-bound style will sound abstract, pompous, and beside the point. It would be insensitive, however, even if it is true, to lecture someone who has just been downsized about "the greatest good for the greatest number." An empathetic style is much more in order. Whether or not there is a "true" ethical theory, there is always a place—or not a place—for certain ethical styles. It is always necessary, in any social institution, to respect the rules. It is always desirable, in any interpersonal setting, to tune in to the other person's perspective and feelings. It is inescapable, for socially and self-conscious creatures like ourselves, that we should care about what others think of us and care, in particular, about how we feel about ourselves, our characters, our virtues.

To insist, however, that the virtuous style is the "correct" view of ethics is itself a misunderstanding of the ethics of virtue. There are many ways of being virtuous, and there are many ways of being ethical. As Tom Peters writes, "In the end, it's up to each of us and each of us alone to figure out who we are and who we are not, and to act more or less consistently on those conclusions."[88]

Conclusion: Looking Forward to Integrity

As we enter the new millennium, there is an overriding question facing global corporate free enterprise, and that is whether the corporations that now or will control and affect so much of the planet's humanity and resources can demonstrate not only their profitability but their integrity. The old quasi-theological arguments still persist, whether multinational corporations and capitalism in general best serve humanity whether corporations and capitalism are good or evil, whether corporations can have a conscience, and whether responsibility can be expected of them. But in the year 2000, all of this is merely academic. Whether or not this is "the end of history," the free enterprise mentality—along with its complement consumerism—now rules the world. Mass markets, economies of scale, and efficiency of distribution call for massive organizations, and the disappearance of national borders, both in practice and in law, leaves the dominance of the global and multinational corporations unchallenged. There will continue to be more or less local government regulations, some necessary and benign, others annoying, and the most powerful governments may take on the most powerful corporations, one by one. But no government can match the collective power of the corporate world, and many governments, including the "superpowers," are largely indebted to the corporations. The future of the world, for at least the next critical century, lies in corporate hands. It is no longer simply "a business question" how these corporations conduct their business and how they conceive of their own identity.

The questions addressed in this book all come together in one great concern, and that is whether and how the virtues and the integrity of the people who make up our corporations and the increasingly international business world can be implemented in that world and in those corporations. I do not doubt that the great majority of managers and executives take their own virtues and sense of integrity very seriously. They want the best from as well as for themselves, and they want the best for as well as from their organizations. They know that it is not a law of nature or of economics that a business must pursue its profits *no matter what*. They know that a corporation has obligations to its loyal employees and to the community that helped it flourish. This is not to preach socialism or to attack the free enterprise system. It is simply to say, what we all know when we go to work each day, that business is a human and a social enterprise. It must take human ends, responsibilities, and concerns as its continuing focus. To say that a corporation has a responsibility to the well-being of its customers and employees, quite apart from the need to preserve brand loyalty and avoid legal liabilities, is not paternalism. It is a simple statement about any human relationship, that we are responsible to one another and responsible in particular for that which we bring about (especially when we profit from it as well).

What blocks these simple truths is a set of stunningly clichéd dogmas. I heard them summarized in one perfectly ordinary sentence by a chamber of commerce spokesperson a few months ago. He said, "What makes this country great is the fact that anyone can start a business and make as much money as they can without having to answer to anyone." (A quick aside, the start-up business he was referring to was the largest industrial corporation in the world.) But "what makes this country great" is not just the fact that anyone can (try to) start a business but a long history of mutual respect and tolerance, a belligerent insistence on individual freedom *combined with* its continuing (if fragile) sense of community and an enormous sense of individual and collective responsibility. Whether one looks to the religious or secular history of the United States, it is evident that along with the ambition to make money there has always been the countervailing wisdom that "money isn't everything," that "money can't buy love or happiness" (despite the many wisecracks to the contrary), that love, friendship, respect, and challenges that allow us to become who we want to be are what make life worthwhile. There are far more things on earth and in heaven than are dreamed of in mere economics, and it is for good reason that businesspeople present themselves as "pillars of the community," not because they have made a lot of money but because they see their success in terms of their contribution to the community and as proof of their own virtues and integrity.

Thinking in terms of "making money" and "the market," devoid of any larger sense of obligation or ethics, never made any country or culture "great." Indeed, such crude self-interested thinking is what marks countries and cultures for destruction. But the argument doesn't really change when it gets shifted to the infamous "obligation to the stockholders." Not a week goes by without some socially destructive corporate act or policy being defended in those terms, as if that single obligation closed the question. But what gives us hope is that the executives of those corporations are for the most part not at all happy with such decisions, even when they feel obliged to make them. And they know full well that their obligation to the stockholders is not exclusive, that it does not eclipse their other obligations, that it does not substitute for their sense of their own integrity or compensate for its loss. But a combination of established dogma, shortsighted legal liabilities, legislative cowardice and corruption, and lack of public awareness, education, and imagination contrive to maintain this singular and ultimately destructive sense of obligation in even the very best CEOs and corporate directors.

It is not for me, a mere philosopher, to suggest the legislative and legal reforms that might change this picture and allow good corporate executives to exercise their best judgment in the corporate decisions that now so profoundly affect the future of humanity. But what I can and will do, as a mere philosopher, is to keep hammering away at what should become increasingly obvious—that in the new global marketplace, free enterprise carries with it all of the responsibilities of freedom, the obligation to be the best that one can be, the obligation to care about others who are also free but perhaps not so fortunate, the obligation to look beyond one's immediate goals to a larger and inevitably shared global future.

References and Recommended Reading

Andrews, Kenneth R., "Can the Best Corporations Be Made Moral?"
Harvard Business Review (May–June 1973).

Andrews, Kenneth R., "Ethics in Practice," *Harvard Business Review*
(Sept.–Oct. 1989).

Andrews, Kenneth R., and C. Roland Christensen, *Business Policy:
Texts and Cases*, 6th ed. (Homewood, IL: Irwin, 1987).

Aristotle, *Nicomachean Ethics* in *The Works of Aristotle*, trans. T. Irwin
(Indianapolis: Hackett, 1985).

Aristotle, *Nicomachean Ethics* book IV, ch. 9, trans. D. Ross (Oxford:
Oxford University Press, 1925).

Aristotle, *Politics*, trans. B. Jowett (New York: Modern Library, 1943).

Arrow, Kenneth, *Social Choice and Individual Values* (New Haven: Yale
University Press, 1963).

Axelrod, Robert, *The Evolution of Cooperation* (New York: Basic
Books, 1984).

Bass, Bernard M., *Leadership and Performance Beyond Expectations*
(New York: Free Press, 1985).

Bellah, Robert, et al., *Habits of the Heart* (Berkeley: University of
California Press, 1985).

Bentham, Jeremy, *Introduction to the Principles of Morals and
Legislation* (London: Athlone, 1970).

Blum, Lawrence A., "Compassion," in A. Rorty, ed., *Explaining
Emotions* (Los Angeles: University of California Press, 1980).

Boatright, John R., *Ethics and the Conduct of Business* (Englewood Cliffs, NJ: Prentice-Hall, 1997).

Bok, Sisela, *Lying* (New York: Random House, 1978).

Bowie, Norman, *Business Ethics* (Englewood Cliffs, NJ: Prentice-Hall, 1982).

Bowie, Norman, "The Profit Seeking Paradox," in N. Dale Wright, ed., *Ethics of Administration* (Provo, UT: Brigham Young University Press, 1988).

Brandeis, Louis, "Competition," *American Legal News* vol. 44 (Jan. 1913).

Burns, James MacGregor, *Leadership* (New York: Harper & Row, 1978).

Carnegie, Andrew, "Wealth," in T. Donaldson and P. Werhane, *Ethical Issues in Business* (Englewood Cliffs, NJ: Prentice-Hall, 1983).

Carr, Alfred, "Is Business Bluffing Ethical?" *Harvard Business Review* (Jan.–Feb. 1968).

Carter, Stephen L., *Integrity* (New York: Basic Books, 1996).

Champy, James, *Reengineering Management: The Mandate for New Leadership* (New York: Harper, 1995).

Ciulla, Joanne, *Ethics, The Heart of Leadership* (Westport, CT: Praeger, 1998).

Ciulla, Joanne, *Honest Work* (New York: Random House, 1999).

Coleman, Jules L., *Markets, Morals and the Law* (Cambridge, UK: Cambridge University Press, 1988).

Collins, Denis, "Aristotle and Business," *Journal of Business Ethics* vol. 6 (1987).

Cooper, John, *Reason and Human Good in Aristotle* (Indianapolis: Hackett, 1977).

Cropsey, Joseph, *Polity and Economy* (Westport, CT: Greenwood, 1957).

Davidson, Greg, and Paul Davidson, *Economics for a Civilized Society* (New York: Norton, 1989).

Deal, Terrence, and Allan Kennedy, *Corporate Cultures* (Reading, MA: Addison-Wesley, 1982).

de George, Richard, *Business Ethics* (New York: Macmillan, 1982).

de George, Richard, *Competing with Integrity in International Business* (New York: Oxford University Press).

de George, Richard, *Ethics, Free Enterprise and Public Policy* (New York: Oxford University Press, 1978).

Denning, Peter, and Robert Metcalfe, *Beyond Calculation* (New York: Springer-Verlag, 1997).

Derry, Robbin, *Moral Reasoning in Organizations: A Study of Men and Women Managers* (Ann Arbor, MI: University Microfilms, 1987).

Dobson, John, *Finance Ethics* (Lanham, MD: Rowman and Littlefield, 1997).

Donaldson, Thomas, *Corporations and Morality* (Englewood Cliffs, NJ: Prentice-Hall, 1982).

Donaldson, Thomas, *International Business Theory* (New York: Oxford University Press, 1990).

Donaldson, T., and P. Werhane, *Ethical Issues in Business* (Englewood Cliffs, NJ: Prentice-Hall, 1983).

Douglas, Mary, *How Institutions Think* (New York: Syracuse University Press, 1986).

Drucker, Peter, "Ethical Chic," *Forbes* (Sept. 14, 1981): 160–173.

Drucker, Peter, *Management* (New York: Harper & Row, 1974).

Dunfee, Thomas, "Business Ethics and Extant Social Contracts," *Business Ethics Quarterly* (Jan. 1991).

Edwards, Owen, *Upward Nobility* (New York: Crown, 1991).

Etzioni, Amitai, *The Moral Dimension: Toward a New Economics* (New York: Free Press, 1989).

Feinberg, Joel, *Social Philosophy* (Englewood Cliffs, NJ: Prentice-Hall 1973).

Fisher, H.A.L., *A History of Europe* vol. 1 (London: Collins, 1935).

Fletcher, George P., *Loyalty* (New York: Oxford University Press, 1993).

Flew, Anthony, "The Profit Motive," *Ethics* vol. 86 (July 1976): 312–322.

Flores, Carlos F., *Management and Communication in the Office of the Future* (Berkeley, CA: Logonet, 1982).

Flores, Fernando, Charles Spinosa, and Hubert Dreyfus, *Disclosing New Worlds* (Cambridge, MA: MIT Press, 1997).

Frank, Robert H., *Passions Within Reason: The Strategic Role of the Emotions* (New York: Norton, 1989).

Freman, R. Edward, ed., *Business Ethics: The State of the Art* (New York: Oxford University Press, 1991).

Freman, R. Edward, and Jeanne Liedtka, "Corporate Social Responsibility: A Critical Approach," in *Business Horizons* vol. 34. no. 4 (1991) pp. 92–98.

Freeman, R. Edward, and D. Gilbert, *Corporate Strategy and the Search for Ethics* (Englewood Cliffs, NJ: Prentice-Hall, 1988).

French, Peter A., *Collective and Corporate Responsibility* (New York: Columbia University Press, 1984).

French, Peter A., "The Corporation as a Moral Person," *American Philosophical Quarterly* 16 (1979): 3.

French, P., T. Uehling, and H. Wettstein, eds., *Ethical Theory: Character and Virtue* (*Midwest Studies in Philosophy* XIII) (Minneapolis: University of Minnesota Press, 1988).

French, P., T. Uehling, and H. Wettstein, eds., *Social and Political Philosophy* (*Midwest Studies in Philosophy* VII) (Minneapolis: University of Minnesota Press, 1982).

Friedman, Milton, "The Social Responsibility of Business Is to Increase Its Profits," *New York Times* (Sept. 13, 1970).

Friedman, Milton, and Rose Friedman, *Free to Choose* (New York: Harcourt Brace Jovanovich, 1979).

Fukuyama, Francis, *Trust: The Social Virtues and the Creation of Prosperity* (New York: Free Press, 1995).

Gautier, David, *Morals by Agreement* (New York: Oxford University Press, 1986).

Geertz, Clifford, *The Interpretation of Cultures* (New York: Basic Books, 1975).

Gellerman, Saul, "Why 'Good' Managers Make Bad Ethical Choices," *Harvard Business Review* (July–Aug. 1986).

Gerber, Michael E., *The E-Myth* (New York: HarperCollins, 1986).

Goodpaster, Kenneth, "Ethical Imperatives and Corporate Leadership," in R. Edward Freeman, ed., *Business Ethics: The State of the Art* (New York: Oxford University Press, 1991).

Goodpaster, K., and J. Mathews, "Can a Corporation Have a Conscience?" *Harvard Business Review* vol. 60, no. 1 (Jan.–Feb. 1982): 132–141.

Gould, Stephen Jay, *Full House: The Spread of Excellence from Plato to Darwin* (New York: Harmony Books, 1996).

Grove, Andrew, *Only Paranoids Survive* (New York: Currency Doubleday, 1996).

Hampshire, Stuart, *Innocence and Experience* (Cambridge, MA: Harvard University Press, 1989).

Hampshire, Stuart, ed., *Public and Private Morality* (Cambridge, UK: Cambridge University Press, 1978)

Hartle, Anthony E., *Moral Issues in Military Decision-Making* (Lawrence: University Press of Kansas, 1989).

Hartman, Edwin, *Organizational Ethics and the Good Life* (New York: Oxford University Press, 1996).

Hazlitt, David V., *Capitalism with Morality* (New York: Oxford University Press, 1996).

Hegel, G.W.F., *The Phenomenology of Spirit*, trans. A. V. Miller (New York: Oxford University Press, 1977).

Hegel, G.W.F., *The Philosophy of Right*, trans. T. Knox (New York: Oxford University Press, 1967).

Hennig, M., and Anne Jardin, *The Managerial Woman* (New York: Doubleday, 1977).

Hirschman, Albert O., *The Passions and the Interests* (Princeton, NJ: Princeton University Press, 1998).

Hobbes, Thomas, *Leviathan* (New York: Hafner, 1926).

Hoffman, Martin L., "Empathetic Emotions and Justice in Society," *Social Justice Research* vol. III, no. 4 (Dec. 1989): 283–311.

Horniman, Alexander B., "Whatever Happened to Loyalty?" *Ethics Digest* (1989).

Hume, David, *A Treatise of Human Nature* (New York: Oxford University Press, 1978).

Jackall, Robert, *Moral Mazes* (New York: Oxford University Press, 1988).

James, Geoffrey, *Business Wisdom of the Electronic Elite* (New York: Random House, 1996).

Jay, Anthony, *Management and Machiavelli* (New York: Holt, Rinehart & Winston, 1968).

Kant, Immanuel, *Grounding of the Metaphysics of Morals*, trans. J. Ellington (Indianapolis: Hackett, 1981).

Kant, Immanuel, *The Metaphysical Elements of Justice*, trans. J. Ladd (Indianapolis: Bobbs-Merrill, 1965).

Keeley, Michael, *A Social Contract Theory of Organizations* (Notre Dame, IN: University of Notre Dame Press, 1988).

Kohn, Alfie, *Beyond Selfishness* (New York: Basic Books, 1990).

Kristol, Irving, "Ethics Anyone? Or Morals?" *Wall Street Journal* (Sept. 15, 1987).

Kristol, Irving, *Two Cheers for Capitalism* (New York: Basic Books, 1978).

Ladd, John, "Morality and the Ideal of Rationality in Formal Organizations," *The Monist* (October 1970).

Lakoff, George, and Mark Johnson, *Metaphors We Live By* (Chicago: University of Chicago Press, 1980).

Lewis, Michael, *Liar's Poker* (New York: Norton, 1989).

Lindholm, Charles, *Charisma* (Oxford, UK: Blackwell, 1991).

Luce, R.D., and Howard Raiffa, *Games and Decisions* (New York: Wiley, 1957).

Luhmann, Niklas, *Trust and Power*, trans H. Davis, J. Raffan, and K. Rooney (New York: Wiley, 1979).

MacIntyre, Alasdair, *After Virtue* (Notre Dame, IN: University of Notre Dame Press, 1981).

MacIntyre, Alasdair, *Whose Justice? Which Rationality?* (Notre Dame, IN: University of Notre Dame Press, 1988).

MacIntyre, Alasdair, "Why Are the Problems of Business Ethics Insoluble?" *Proceedings of the First National Conference on Business Ethics* (Waltham, MA: Bentley College, 1977).

Maister, David H., *Passionate Professionalism* (New York: Free Press, 1997).

Marx, Karl, *Selected Writings*, ed. David McClellan (New York: Oxford University Press, 1977).

Mayeroff, Milton, *On Caring* (New York: Harper & Row, 1971).

McCoy, Bowen H., "The Parable of the Sadhu," *Harvard Business Review* (1984).

McFall, Lynne, "Integrity," *Ethics* (October 1987).

McGregor, Douglas A., *The Human Side of Enterprise* (New York: McGraw-Hill, 1960).

Mencius, *Mencius on the Mind*, trans. D.C. Lau (New York: Penguin, 1970).

Menken, Daniel L., *Faith, Hope, and the Corporation* (St. Paul, MN: Phrontisterian, 1988).

Mill, John Stuart, *Utilitarianism* (Indianapolis: Hackett, 1981).

Moorthy, R.S., *Uncompromising Integrity* (Schaumburg, IL: Motorola University Press, 1997).

Murray, Patrick, *Reflections on Commercial Life* (London: Routledge, 1997).

Naisbett, John, *Re-inventing the Corporation* (New York: Warner, 1985).

Nietzsche, Friedrich, *Genealogy of Morals*, trans. W. Kaufmann (New York: Random House, 1967).

Nietzsche, Friedrich, *Thus Spoke Zarathustra*, trans. W. Kaufmann (New York: Viking, 1954).

Noddings, Nell, *Caring* (Los Angeles: University of California Press, 1984).

Nonaka, I., and H. Takeuchi, *The Knowledge-Creating Company* (New York: Oxford University Press, 1995).

Nozick, Robert, *Anarchy, State and Utopia* (New York: Basic Books, 1974).

Nozick, Robert, *Philosophical Explanations* (New York: Simon & Schuster, 1990).

Obst, Lynda Rosen, *Hello, He Lied* (Boston: Little, Brown, 1996).

Ohmae, Kenichi, *The Borderless World* (New York: HarperCollins, 1991).

Paskin, Mark, *The Hard Problems of Management* (San Francisco: Jossey-Bass, 1986).

Payne, Lynne Sharp, "Ethics as Character Development," in R. Edward Freeman, ed., *Business Ethics: The State of the Art* (New York: Oxford University Press, 1991).

Peters, Tom, "The Ethics Debate," *Ethics Digest* (Dec. 1989).

Pincoffs, Edmund, *Quandaries and Virtues* (Lawrence: University Press of Kansas, 1986).

Plato, *Republic*, trans. C. Grube (Indianapolis: Hackett, 1974).

Rawls, John, *A Theory of Justice* (Cambridge, MA: Harvard University Press, 1971).

Reichheld, Frederick, *The Loyalty Effect* (Cambridge, MA: Harvard Business School Press, 1996).

Rescher, Nicholas, *Unselfishness* (Pittsburgh: University of Pittsburgh Press, 1975).

Roberts, Wess, *Leadership Secrets of Attila the Hun* (New York: Warner Books, 1989).

Roberts, Wess, *Victory Secrets of Attila the Hun* (New York: Warner Books, 1993).

Royce, Josiah, *The Philosophy of Loyalty* (New York: Macmillan, 1908).

Rubin, Harriett, *The Princessa* (New York: Doubleday, 1997).

Samuelson, Robert J., "Competition: Tried and True," *Newsweek* (June 11, 1990).

Sandel, Michael, *Liberalism and the Limits of Justice* (New York: Cambridge University Press, 1982).

Sartre, Jean-Paul, *Being and Nothingness* part III. ch. 4 (New York: Simon & Schuster, 1956).

Scheff, Thomas, "Socialization of Emotions: Pride and Shame As Causal Agents," in T. Kemper, ed., *Research Agendas in the Sociology of Emotions* (Albany: SUNY Press, 1990).

Sen, Amartya, *On Ethics and Economics* (Oxford, UK: Blackwell, 1989).

Singer, Peter, *Practical Ethics* (Cambridge, UK: Cambridge University Press, 1979).

Smith, Adam, *An Inquiry into the Nature and Causes of the Wealth of Nations* (New York: Hafner, 1948).

Smith, Adam, *The Theory of Moral Sentiments* (London: George Bell, 1880).

Solomon, Robert C., *Above the Bottom Line* (New York: Harcourt Brace, 1994).

Solomon, Robert C., *It's Good Business* (Lanham, MD: Rowman and Littlefield, 1998).

Solomon, Robert C., *A Passion for Justice* (Reading, MA: Addison-Wesley, 1990).

Solomon, Robert C., *The Passions* (Indianapolis: Hackett, 1993).

Stone, Christopher, *Where the Law Ends: The Social Control of Corporate Behavior* (New York: Harper & Row, 1975).

Taylor, Gabriele, *Pride, Shame, and Guilt* (Oxford, UK: Clarendon, 1985).

Thomas, Laurence, *On Being Moral* (Philadelphia: Temple University Press, 1989).

Townsend, Robert, *Up the Organization* (New York: Knopf, 1970).

Ungar, Robert, *Passion: An Essay on Personality* (New York: Free Press, 1984).

Velasquez, Manuel G., *Business Ethics* (Englewood Cliffs, NJ: Prentice-Hall, 1982).

von Neumann, John, and Oskar Morgenstern, *Theory of Games and Economic Behavior* (New York: Wiley, 1944).

Walton, Clarence C., *The Moral Manager* (Cambridge, MA: Ballinger, 1988).

Walzer, Michael, *Spheres of Justice* (New York: Harper & Row, 1983).

Weber, Max, *From Max Weber*, eds. H.H. Gerth and C. Wright Mills (New York: Oxford University Press, 1946).

Weber, Max, *Theory of Social and Economic Organization*, trans. A. Henderson and T. Parsons (Glencoe, NY: Free Press, 1947).

Werhane, Patricia, *Ethics and Economics: The Legacy of Adam Smith for Modern Capitalism* (New York: Oxford University Press, 1991).

Whyte, David, *The Heart Aroused* (New York: Doubleday, 1994).

Williams, Bernard, *Morality* (New York: Harper & Row, 1972).

Williams, Bernard, *Moral Luck* (Cambridge, UK: Cambridge University Press, 1981).

Notes

1   *Harvard Business Review* MTI videos, E. McCoy, "Parable of Sadhu" (1984).
2   Stephen Jay Gould, *Full House: The Spread of Excellence from Plato to Darwin* (New York: Harmony Books, 1996), p. 7.
3   Andrew Grove, *Only Paranoids Survive* (New York: Currency Doubleday, 1996).
4   Wess Roberts, *Leadership Secrets of Attila the Hun* (New York: Warner Books, 1989), and *Victory Secrets of Attila the Hun* (New York: Warner Books, 1993).
5   Roberts, *Victory Secrets*, p. 36.
6   Roberts, *Victory Secrets*, p. 127.
7   H.A.L. Fisher, *A History of Europe* vol. 1 (London: Collins, 1935), p. 131.
8   Anthony Jay, *Management and Machiavelli* (New York: Holt, Rinehart & Winston, 1968).
9   Harriett Rubin, *The Princessa* (New York: Doubleday, 1997).
10 Thomas Hobbes, *Leviathan* (1651).
11 Frank Rich, "Mickey Mouse Clubbed," *New York Times* (Friday, Dec. 13, 1996).
12 Michael Ryan, "They Call Their Boss a Hero," *Parade Magazine* (Sept. 8, 1996): 4–5.
13 Roberts, *Victory Secrets*, p. xvi.

14   Alfred Carr, "Is Business Bluffing Ethical?" *Harvard Business Review* (Jan.–Feb. 1968).

15   Francis Ford Coppola, *The Godfather* (1972), book by Mario Puzo (Greenwich, CT: Fawcett, 1969).

16   See, for example, the anthropologist Clifford Geertz, *The Interpretation of Cultures* (New York: Basic Books, 1971).

17   Michael Crichton, *Rising Sun* (New York: Knopf, 1992). The phrase does have considerable currency in current-day Japanese business. My thanks to Hiro Umezu for discussion on this.

18   Jerry Useem, "Internet Superstart Enlists Locals to Battle Giants," *Inc.* (Oct. 1996): 17.

19   Geofferey James, *Business Wisdom of the Electronic Elite* (New York: Random House, 1996), p. 29.

20   Anthony E. Hartle, *Moral Issues in Military Decision-Making* (Lawrence: University Press of Kansas, 1989), with reference to Bengt Abrahamsson, *Military Professionalism and Political Power* (Beverly Hills: Sage, 1972).

21   James, *The Electronic Elite*, pp. 35–40.

22   Justice Louis Brandeis, "Competition," *American Legal News* vol. 44 (Jan. 1913).

23   Oddly, Michael Hammer and James Champy, best known for the "reengineering" metaphor, are both harsh critics of the "corporate machine" metaphor. Thus they remind us just how entrenched these images are. See Michael Hammer, *Reengineering the Corporation* (New York: Harper Business, 1993), and James Champy, *Reengineering Management: The Mandate for New Leadership* (New York: Harper: 1995).

24   Adam Smith's *Wealth of Nations* was published in 1776. Other best-sellers of the time included Baron d'Holbach's *System of Nature* (published in London in 1759) and Julien le Mettrie's *Man the Machine* (1747).

25   *Business Week* (May 4, 1998).

26   I. Nonaka and H. Takeuchi, *The Knowledge-Creating Company* (New York: Oxford University Press, 1995).

27   James, *The Electronic Elite* (op. cit.).

28   Robert Frank, *The Winner-Take-All Society* (New York: Free Press, 1995).

29   John von Neumann and Oscar Morgenstern, *Theory of Games and Economic Behavior* (New York: Wiley, 1944).

30   *San Francisco Chronicle* (March 31, 1997).

31   *Wall Street Journal* (July 25, 1996).

32   Michael E. Gerber has similarly attacked what he calls the "E-myth" in his book *The E-Myth* (New York: HarperCollins, 1986).

33   Fernando Flores, Charles Spinosa, and Hubert Dreyfus, *Disclosing New Worlds* (Cambridge, MA: MIT Press, 1997).

34   Solomon, *Ethics and Excellence*, pp. 74ff.

35   Flores, Spinosa, and Dreyfus, *Disclosing New Worlds* (op. cit.).

36   As reported in my *A Passion for Justice* (Reading, MA: Addison-Wesley, 1990).

37   Milton Friedman, "The Social Responsibility of Business Is to Increase Its Profits," *New York Times* (Sept. 13, 1970).

38   Peter Drucker, *Management* (New York: Harper & Row, 1974).

39   Anthony Flew, "The Profit Motive," *Ethics* vol. 86 (July 1976): 312–322.

40   Flew, *The Profit Motive*, p. 314.

41   Drucker, *Management*, p. 60.

42   Norman Bowie, "The Profit-Seeking Paradox," in N. Dale Wright, ed., *Ethics of Administration* (Provo, UT: Brigham Young University Press, 1988).

43   Doug Todd, "Recognizing Ethics in Action: Virtue Has Its Own Awards," *Vancouver Sun* (June 15, 1996): D20 (commentary of the 1996 Ethics in Action awards, Vancouver, British Columbia).

44   Stephen L. Carter, *Integrity* (New York: Basic Books, 1996).

45   This distinction between following and "making one's own" is the central tenet of many existentialist philosophies. The nineteenth-century Danish philosopher Søren Kierkegaard thus distinguished between "Christendom," which involved unthinking obedience to Christian beliefs and values, and truly becoming a Christian, which involved a passionate personal commitment. So, too, more recently Martin Heidegger in Germany and Jean-Paul Sartre in France insisted on resolution and authenticity rather than mere rule-following. And although none of them use the word as we do,

one might well summarize this aspect of their philosophies by calling it "integrity."

46 Aristotle and many other ancient ethicists defended this thesis under the rubric of "the unity of the virtues." One flaw tends to lead to others, whereas the virtues tend to reinforce one another.

47 For these prototypes, see Martin Berman's excellent book on compromise, *Splitting the Difference* (Lawrence: University Press of Kansas, 1990), esp. Chapter 3.

48 Mark Paskin, *The Hard Problems of Management* (San Francisco: Jossey-Bass, 1986).

49 Ibid., p. 144.

50 Norman Bowie, "Business Ethics as a Discipline: The Search for Legitimacy," in R. Edward Freeman, ed., *Business Ethics: The State of the Art* (New York: Oxford University Press, 1991), pp. 17–41.

51 See, for example, Robert J. Samuelson in *Newsweek* (May 14, 1990).

52 Bowie, "Business Ethics as a Discipline: The Search for Legitimacy," in R. Edward Freeman, ed., *Business Ethics: The State of the Art* (Oxford University Press, 1991), pp. 17–41.

53 Bowie, "The Profit Seeking Paradox," in *Ethics of Administration*, in N. Dale Wright, ed. (Provo, UT: Brigham Young University, 1988).

54 Robert Jackall, *Moral Mazes* (New York: Oxford University Press, 1988), p. 3.

55 I am indebted in this section to Joanne Ciulla and the Kellogg Foundation for Leadership Studies Project for allowing me to borrow from work I did for them. *Ethics, The Heart of Leadership* (West Port, CT: Praeger Press, 1998).

56 Ernest Greenwood, "Attributes of a Profession," in S. Nosow and W. Form, eds., *Man, Work and Society* (New York: Basic Books, 1962), p. 206. Quoted in Hartle, *Moral Issues in Military Decision-Making*, p. 40.

57 Max Weber, "The Sociology of Charismatic Authority," in H.H. Gerth and C. Wright Mills, eds., *From Max Weber* (New York: Oxford University Press, 1946), pp. 245ff.

58 Robert Nozick, *Philosophical Explanations* (New York: Simon & Schuster, 1990).

59 James MacGregor Burns, *Leadership* (New York: Harper & Row, 1978), p. 243.

60 Bernard M. Bass, *Leadership and Performance Beyond Expectations* (New York: Free Press, 1985).

61 Cult leaders Jim Jones and David Koresh are examples. If it were not for the ultimately lethal consequences, would such figures have ever been noted as "leaders"?

62 Max Weber, *Theory of Social and Economic Organization*, A. Henderson and T. Parsons, trans. (Glencoe, NY: Free Press, 1947).

63 *American Heritage Electronic Dictionary* (Boston: Houghton Mifflin, 1992).

64 I have benefited from several excellent books in the field: Ron Heifitz, *Leadership Without Easy Answers*; Jay A. Conger, *The Charismatic Leader*; and, of course, James MacGregor Burns's classic, *Leadership* (op. cit.).

65 *Wall Street Journal* (March 19, 1997).

66 Lynda Rosen Obst, *Hello, He Lied* (Boston: Little, Brown, 1996).

67 A metaphor he used exactly once in the whole of *Wealth of Nations* (and once prior in his *Theory of the Moral Sentiments*).

68 Michael Lewis, *Liar's Poker* (New York: Norton, 1989).

69 See Frithjof Bergmann, "The Experience of Values," in S. Hauerwas and A. Macintyre, eds., *Revisions* (Notre Dame: Notre Dame University Press, 1983), pp. 127–159.

70 Milton Mayeroff, *On Caring* (New York: Harper & Row, 1971).

71 Mencius, *Mencius on the Mind*, D.C. Lau, trans. (New York: Penguin, 1970).

72 Terrence Deal and Allan Kennedy, *Corporate Cultures* (Reading, MA: Addison-Wesley, 1982).

73 See, for example, Ezra Bowen's essay on business and literacy, "The Rule of Business in Three Levels of Literacy," in Freeman, ed., *Business Ethics: The State of the Art*, where he says, "the fact is that ethics, or accountability, comes in two decorator colors: black and white" (p. 186). For a good

rebuttal, I recommend Joanne Ciulla's reply, which follows Bowen's piece.

74   President Nixon's "peace with honor" in Vietnam meant "avoid political humiliation."

75   *Monty Python* once presented a skit entitled "The Village Idiots' Convention."

76   Deal and Kennedy, *Corporate Cultures* (op. cit.).

77   John Rawls, *A Theory of Justice* (Cambridge, MA: Harvard University Press, 1971), p. 3.

78   Robert Townsend, *Up the Organization* (New York: Knopf, 1970), p. 43.

79   Socrates asks it, as the leading theme of Plato's *Republic*.

80   Alexander B. Horniman, *Ethics Digest* (1989). For two good philosophical discussions of loyalty, see Josiah Royce, *The Philosophy of Loyalty* (New York: Macmillan, 1908) and George P. Fletcher, *Loyalty* (New York: Oxford University Press, 1993).

81   John Rawls, *A Theory of Justice*, part III. Not all societies are honor societies and not everyone's self-esteem is tied to their sense of honor. But shame is not, as Rawls says, failing to live up to one's potential; it is, much more specifically, failing to live up to the standards of the group through which one gains one's self-identity. But, then, failing to live up to one's potential may itself be equivalent to failing to live up to the standards of the group.

82   *Newsweek* (May 6, 1991): 54.

83   Gabrielle Taylor, *Shame, Guilt and Pride* (Oxford, UK: Clarendon, 1985).

84   See, for example, Stuart Hampshire, ed., *Public and Private Morality* (Cambridge, UK: Cambridge University Press, 1978), and his *Innocence and Experience* (Cambridge, MA: Harvard University Press, 1989). See also Bernard Williams, "Politics and Moral Character," in his *Moral Luck* (Cambridge, UK: Cambridge University Press, 1981), and Thomas Nagel, "Ruthlessness in Public Life," in Hampshire, *Public and Private Morality* (op. cit.).

85   Francis Fukuyama, *Trust: The Social Virtues and the Creation of Prosperity* (New York: Free Press, 1995).

86   Niklas Luhmann, *Trust and Power*, p. 80; Bernard Barber,
     Logic and Limits of Trust (New Brunswick, NJ: Rutgers
     University Press, 1983), pp. 2, 71.
87   Friedrich Nietzsche, *Thus Spoke Zarathustra*, W. Kaufmann,
     trans. (New York: Viking, 1954), book 1, 5.
88   Tom Peters, "The Ethics Debate," *Ethics Digest* (Dec. 1989): 2.

Index